LIFE SAVER

W9-BAH-075

THE
ULTIMATE
DEVOTIONAL
HANDBOOK

FOR TEENS

LIFE SAVER

TO SAVE A LIFE

THE ULTIMATE DEVOTIONAL HANDBOOK

FOR TEENS

OVER **50** TOPICS TO HELP YOU GROW IN FAITH
AND SHARE GOD'S LOVE

OUTREACH®

Outreach, Inc.
Vista, CA 92081
www.outreach.com

Writing by Todd Hafer, Vicki Kuyper, Michael Klassen,
and Vicki Caruana in association with
Snapdragon Group℠, Tulsa, OK
Project Management and Editorial Services by
Snapdragon Group℠, Tulsa, OK

ISBN: 978-1-9355-4121-9

Cover Design: Tim Downs
Interior Design: Tim Downs

Printed in the United States of America

When you're in over your head,

I'll be there with you.

When you're in rough waters,

you will not go down.

When you're between a rock

and a hard place,

it won't be a dead end—

Because I am God, your personal God.

Isaiah 43:2–3 MSG

CONTENTS

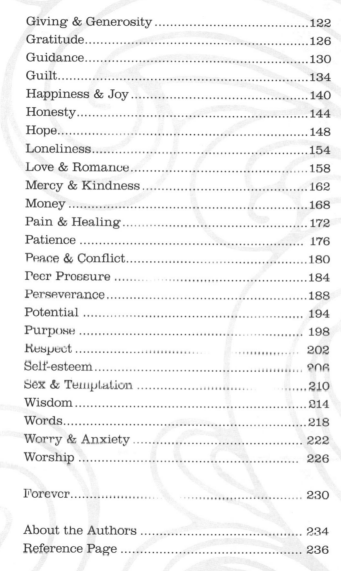

INTRODUCTION

Do you ever hear adults talk about how much the world has changed? Sometimes they long for "simpler times." One thing is for sure: Your world, today's world, is loaded with challenges teens have to face every day. There's so much to deal with: parents, peer pressure, school, dating, your future, your friends, your enemies, your soul. With all the changes going on all around you—and inside you— it's no wonder teens can feel like they're drowning.

This handbook has been created to serve kind of like a life saver—something you can grab onto when the waves of life get high and the seas get choppy. In these pages you will find some answers, some inspiration and some clear thinking in the middle of life's chaos. We've included verses from the Bible—the ultimate handbook for life—along with earthly wisdom from people who've faced some rough waves and made it safely to shore. There are also stories from teens just like you who found strength and hope through God's love and grace.

Most of all, we hope you get to know the One that wants to give you hope for your future, light for your darkness, and comfort for your pain—no matter where you sail on life's journey. We hope you get to know the real Life Saver: Jesus Christ.

Todd H., Vicki K., Mike K., and Vicki C

ACCEPTANCE
DEEPER THAN THE OCEAN

Accept one another, then, just as Christ accepted you, in order to bring praise to God.

Romans 15:7

Right here, right now, God accepts you just the way you are. Morning breath, a bad hair day, or wacky mood swings don't scare Him off. He knows everything about you, even the things you may have been too afraid to tell those closest to you. No matter what you've said or done, you can trust that God will never turn His back on you or walk away. When you reach out to God, He reaches right back—and never lets go.

That doesn't mean God doesn't care about the choices you make. If you really care about your friends, you want them to live happy, healthy lives. The same is true with God. He not only accepts the real you, He also loves you and cares deeply about what happens to you. Even in your wildest dreams, you can't image the depth of His love. It's deeper than the deepest ocean, stretching way beyond the time between your first and last breaths. He wants to help you become the incredible person He created you to be.

That's not all. Knowing that God totally accepts you can help you accept others more easily. If God sees something worth loving in every person you meet, why shouldn't you? You don't have to become BFFs with every random stranger who happens your way. But with God's help, you can learn to accept people for who they are. Just remind yourself, "This is someone God loves." Then, ask God's help in learning to love others the way He loves you, from the inside out.

CATCHING THE WAVE

When a teacher accepts your homework, that acceptance usually comes with conditions. Perhaps the paper has to be five pages in length, be handwritten, or include a bibliography. If you don't follow the instructions, chances are you'll receive a less than stellar grade. Or maybe your assignment will simply be returned as "unacceptable." God's acceptance is different. You don't have to be smart enough, cool enough, fashionable enough, or good-looking enough. He sees your heart, and He accepts you just the way you are.

SURFING FOR WISDOM

GOD judges persons differently than humans do. Men and women look at the face; GOD looks into the heart.
1 Samuel 16:7 MSG

He chose us in Him before the foundation of the world ... according to the good pleasure of His will, to the praise of the glory of His grace, by which He made us accepted in the Beloved.
Ephesians 1:4-6 NKJV

Peter began to speak to them: "I truly understand that God shows no partiality, but in every nation anyone who fears him and does what is right is acceptable to him."
Acts 10:34-35 NRSV

Jesus said, "He who receives you receives me, and he who receives me receives the one who sent me."
Matthew 10:40

LIFE SAVER

DIVING FOR UNDERSTANDING

Give love and unconditional acceptance
to those you encounter, and notice what happens.
Wayne Dyer

Truly loving another means letting go
of all expectations. It means full acceptance,
even celebration of another's personhood.
Anonymous

The art of acceptance is the art of making someone
who has just done you a small favor wish that he might
have done you a greater one.
Russell Lynes

LIFE SAVER CHALLENGE

I will become more accepting of myself and others by:

1. Refusing to make snap judgments about people based on their looks and how they dress.

2. Remembering that God finds something to love in every person.

3. Remembering that God took great care to create each person as a one-of-a-kind work of art.

MANNING THE LIFE BOAT

Think of someone you know who seems to have a hard time fitting in. Reach out and make an effort to get to know that person better. Sit down next to that person at lunch; walk together to class. Give someone the gift of acceptance, and you may find you've made a special friend

SAIL ON IN PRAYER

Lord God,
Thank You that You know me
and love me, inside and out.
I'm so glad I never have to pretend with You.
You accept me for who I really am. Help me share more
and more of myself with You—the good and the bad.
Teach me how to accept others the
same way You've accepted me.
Amen.

ANGER
CALMING TROUBLED WATERS

Bridle your anger, trash your wrath, cool your pipes—it only makes things worse.

Psalm 37:8 MSG

This means war, thought Edwin Stanton. And Stanton *knew* war. He was the United States' Secretary of War during the violent and bloody Civil War.

The target of Stanton's anger was a Union general whom he felt was defying authority. Stanton shared his anger with his boss, President Abraham Lincoln. Lincoln suggested Stanton write a letter to the Union general expressing his feelings.

Stanton obeyed. His pen was like a hypodermic needle, injecting every drop of anger into a scathing letter. Proudly, he returned to Lincoln. The president read what Stanton had written. Then he said, "You don't want to send this letter. You should put it in the stove and write the general *another* one. That's what I do."

One of President Lincoln's hallmarks was his wisdom. And he was wise enough to know that anger is a dangerous emotion. Angry people say things they don't mean. Think about Lincoln the next time you're typing an angry email or preparing to call someone and rip into him or her. Then save a draft of that email and come back to it later, when you're no longer boiling inside. Or, before you start shouting at someone, stop and think about what you're doing.

This approach to handling anger is not just presidential; it's biblical. The Bible says, "In your anger do not sin" (Ephesians 4:26). Everyone gets angry. The key to healthy relationships is *how* we handle it. So, if you *have* to blow off steam, go ahead. Just make sure no one gets burned in the process.

CATCHING THE WAVE

Anger is called "a secondary emotion." This doesn't mean it's unimportant. It just means anger springs from some other emotion or state of mind. Frustration. Humiliation. Jealousy. Pain. This knowledge can be extremely helpful—both in dealing with your own anger and understanding anger in others.

So if one of your friends says something cruel to you, call a time-out. Consider why the statement made you mad. Because it hurt your feelings? Because it embarrassed you? Digging a little deeper can help you resist the urge to hurt back and continue an angry battle that will quickly kill your friendship.

SURFING FOR WISDOM

A gentle answer turns away wrath, but a harsh word stirs up anger.
Proverbs 15:1

Go ahead and be angry. You do well to be angry—but don't use your anger as fuel for revenge. And don't stay angry. Don't go to bed angry. Don't give the Devil that kind of foothold in your life.
Ephesians 4:26-27 MSG

Everyone should be quick to listen, slow to speak and slow to become angry, for man's anger does not bring about the righteous life that God desires.
James 1:19-20

Angry people stir up a lot of discord.
Proverbs 29:22 MSG

DIVING FOR UNDERSTANDING

For every minute you are angry,
you lose sixty seconds of happiness.
Ralph Waldo Emerson

Anger is only one letter short of danger.
Anonymous

Speak when you are angry and you will make the best speech you will ever regret.
Ambrose Bierce

LIFE SAVER CHALLENGE

I will manage my anger
with these steps:

1. I will stop, think, and pray before expressing my anger.

2. If I simply must vent my anger, I will do it in private.

3. I will plan and rehearse difficult conversations before having them—or walk away from heated arguments until I have my temper under control.

4. I will let angry emails sit awhile before sending them.

5. I won't text or instant-message when I'm angry.

MANNING THE LIFE BOAT

If you are looking for ways to share Jesus' love with the people around you—and demonstrate that Jesus' followers are different from the crowd—keeping a lid on your temper is a great place to start. When you feel yourself losing your cool, step back. Ask God to help you demonstrate to others what God is doing in your life.

SAIL ON IN PRAYER

Dear God,
I'm only human.
Sometimes I get mad,
just like everyone else.
Please help me manage my anger
wisely and maturely.
And help me to be more understanding,
more patient, and more helpful
as I deal with the anger of the
people around me.
Amen.

APPEARANCE
JUST BENEATH THE WATER'S SURFACE

Man looks at the outward appearance, but the LORD looks at the heart.
1 Samuel 16:7 NKJV

"So ... how did it go? Did you have a good time?" Briana asked her best friend the day after prom.

"It wasn't what I expected," Ann began.

"What do you mean? You couldn't wait to go to prom with Michael. You waited all semester for him to ask you. You guys look so good together," Briana said.

"We may have looked good, but it sure didn't feel good. I take that back—it didn't feel good to me." Ann burst into tears as she told her best friend how this handsome, smart, and supposedly good guy kept grabbing her inappropriately in public at the prom. She was humiliated. He wasn't such a good guy after all.

There are all kinds of people in the world. Some are as beautiful inside as they are on the outside. Some are not so beautiful on the outside, but they are kind and good and shine like a precious jewel on the inside. And some people are jellyfish. These exquisite sea creatures live just beneath the surface of the water. Many people are attracted to their beauty, only to realize too late that they pack a painful sting.

People aren't always who they appear to be. It's important to consider more than what a person looks like before trusting him or her with the most precious part of yourself—your heart. Ask God to help you notice what counts—how that person treats others, what that person says and does. That's where the truth lies.

CATCHING THE WAVE

The Bible says that God doesn't consider the outer appearance of a person; He sees what's in the heart. Ask God to reveal the real character of a person to you and then get the water out of your eyes and ears. Watch for spontaneous kindness and listen for truthful words. These are the true signs of inner beauty. And be kind to yourself as well.

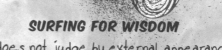

SURFING FOR WISDOM

God does not judge by external appearance.
Galatians 2:6

What matters is not your outer appearance—the styling of your hair, the jewelry you wear, the cut of your clothes—but your inner disposition.
1 Peter 3:3-4 MSG

Women who claim to be devoted to God should make themselves attractive by the good things they do.
1 Timothy 2:10 NLT

Charm can mislead and beauty soon fades. The woman to be admired and praised is the woman who lives in the Fear-of-GOD.
Proverbs 31:30 MSG

DIVING FOR UNDERSTANDING

It is only with the heart that one can see clearly,
for the most essential things
are invisible to the eye.
Antoine de Saint-Exupéry

You don't love someone for their looks, or their clothes, or for
their fancy car, but because they sing a song only you can hear.
Anonymous

Appearances are often deceiving.
Aesop

LIFE SAVER CHALLENGE

I will focus more on inward appearances by:

1. Asking God to reveal the true heart of each person I meet.

2. Getting to know people before committing myself to them.

3. Checking my reflection and asking myself, "Can people see who I really am when they look at me?"

MANNING THE LIFE BOAT

We sometimes get used to hanging only with people who look like us. God asks that we reach out to those we normally wouldn't. Name two people you could sit with at lunch that you wouldn't have thought to sit with before.

1.

2.

SAIL ON IN PRAYER

Lord,
I want what I look like
to reflect who I am inside.
I want to give my heart to others
based on who You show me they are, not on
who they appear to be.
Give me the courage to step outside my comfort zone
and welcome into my inner circle those who
don't fit my mold. You know our hearts.
Help me to remember
that is what really connects us.
Amen.

AUTHORITY
FOLLOWING THE CAPTAIN

Obey your leaders and submit to their authority. They keep watch over you.
Hebrews 13:17

Ming Kipa, a Nepalese Sherpa, holds the title for the youngest person to climb Mount Everest. She was just 15 years old when she set the record! Often called the "ceiling of the world," Mount Everest sits between the borders of China and Nepal, 29,029 feet above sea level.

While Ming deserves a great deal of credit for achieving such a challenging and dangerous record, those who helped her along the way should be recognized as well. Not only did her 24-year-old brother join her on the expedition, but her sister Lhakpa did as well. Lhakpa had successfully climbed the mountain three times. Would Ming have been able to accomplish her amazing feat without an experienced climber by her side? Maybe so, but probably not.

Like Ming, you're climbing a challenging and dangerous mountain for the first time—a mountain called life. Without the guidance and instruction of the responsible adults in your life—parents, teachers, church leaders, even law enforcement officers—your chances of successfully scaling the mountain greatly decrease. God has placed authority in your life for a purpose. He wants you to successfully avoid the great dangers that confront you on every side.

One day Ming may be the one who leads a less experienced climber up the mountain. And one day you will be the parent, the teacher, the mentor, the pastor. It will be you in that position of authority. Until then, listen closely and honor those whom God has entrusted to see you safely up the mountain.

CATCHING THE WAVE

When God created the heavens and the earth, the Bible tells us the earth was "formless and empty" (Genesis 1:2). In other words, it was a jumbled-up mess. Since the beginning, God has been creating order out of chaos. That's His intent with the world you live in, but it's also His intent with your life. Respecting the authorities God has placed over you brings order out of chaos. This doesn't mean that God has given anyone the right to treat you in ways that are against the law or God's Word. However, respecting and cooperating with those who have authority over your life will help you navigate a safe passage.

SURFING FOR WISDOM

I urge, then, first of all, that requests, prayers, intercession and thanksgiving be made for everyone—for kings and all those in authority, that we may live peaceful and quiet lives in all godliness and holiness.

1 Timothy 2:1-2

Be submissive to those who are older. All of you, clothe yourselves with humility toward one another, because, "God opposes the proud but gives grace to the humble." Humble yourselves, therefore, under God's mighty hand, that he may lift you up.

1 Peter 5:5-6

If you honor your father and mother, "things will go well for you, and you will have a long life on the earth."

Ephesians 6:3 NLT

The authorities do not strike fear in people who are doing right, but in those who are doing wrong .... Do what is right, and they will honor you.

Romans 13:3 NLT

LIFE SAVER

DIVING FOR UNDERSTANDING

Obedience to lawful authority
is the foundation
of manly character.
Robert E. Lee

The highest duty is to respect authority.
Leo XIII

If you accept the authority of Jesus in your life,
then you accept the authority of his words.
Colin Urquhart

LIFE SAVER CHALLENGE

I will show that I honor those in authority over me by:

1. Living within the boundaries my parents, teachers, and other authorities have placed on my life, knowing that those boundaries are there to protect me.

2. Showing respect to those people—when they are present and when they aren't.

3. Spending time with those in authority so I can better understand what it's like to be in a position of authority.

4. Writing a thank-you note or e-mail to someone who is an authority figure and has made a difference in my life.

MANNING THE LIFE BOAT

Respecting and obeying those in authority over you is much easier when your friends are doing the same. Name two ways you can help your friends recognize the importance of respect for authority:

1.

2.

SAIL ON IN PRAYER

Dear God,
Thank You for giving me people
who protect and guide me.
I admit, though, that sometimes I don't feel
like respecting or obeying them.
Help me see my life from their perspective
and give me the strength to live
within their boundaries ...
even when I don't feel like it.
Amen.

BALANCE
CHARTING A SMOOTH COURSE

Our lives get in step with God and all others by letting him set the pace.
Romans 3:28 MSG

Learning to juggle is hard work. Just ask Wesley Peden, the world's best teen juggler. Wesley learned to juggle at age five by following the example of his juggling dad. At 14, Wesley won the junior division of the 2010 International Juggling Competition. For a pro like Wesley, juggling apples and rubber balls is considered kid stuff. He prefers juggling bowling balls, knives, and yo-yos.

But Wesley has nothing on you. You have to juggle school, friendships, chores, homework, eating, sleeping, down time, and time with God—and that's just for starters. How do you juggle them all without letting anything drop?

Planning, prayer, and keeping your priorities in line help balance a busy life. Balancing your priorities simply means making sure that what matters to you lines up with what matters to God. Things like purpose (getting a good education so you can succeed in a career that fits well with the person God created you to be), relationships (learning to love your family, friends, and God more each day), and health (taking good care of the amazing body you've been given) should be high on that list. The higher the priority, the more time these areas should receive in your schedule.

As for planning your day, try making two lists: what you have to do and what you want to do. Once you've checked off List One, freely enjoy List Two. Just remember to leave room for the unexpected. A flat tire, the flu, or last-minute movie invitations happen. God keeps the whole universe in balance, so don't hesitate to call on Him for help. Pray as you plan and prioritize. You too can become a juggling pro.

CATCHING THE WAVE

When life is busy, you have a couple of options. You can over-commit to the point of burnout. You can get so overwhelmed that you give up and drop out. Or you can ask God to help you find balance. A balanced life is a healthy, God-honoring life. It's the kind of life Jesus lived. He spent His days teaching, healing, and helping those around Him. But Jesus also took time out. He dined with friends, went to a wedding, and climbed a mountain just to spend time alone with His Father. Want to follow Jesus? Follow His example by putting first things first and keeping your priorities clear.

SURFING FOR WISDOM

Oh, that my steps might be steady, keeping to the course you set.
Psalm 119:5 MSG

Listen for God's voice in everything you do, everywhere you go; he's the one who will keep you on track.
Proverbs 3:6 MSG

Keep your eyes straight ahead; ignore all sideshow distractions. Watch your step, and the road will stretch out smooth before you.
Proverbs 4:25–27 MSG

Let all things be done decently and in order.
1 Corinthians 14:40 NKJV

DIVING FOR UNDERSTANDING

Live a balanced life—learn some and think some and draw and paint and sing and dance and play and work every day some.
Robert Fulghum

When our life is out of balance we have stress! Balance in your life does bring less stress to your life!
Catherine Pulsifer

Just as your car runs more smoothly and requires less energy to go faster and farther when the wheels are in perfect alignment, you perform better when your thoughts, feelings, emotions, goals, and values are in balance.
Brian Tracy

LIFE SAVER CHALLENGE

I will find a better balance in my life with these five steps:

1. Saying "no" when asked to do something I know I don't have time for.
2. Doing tasks I dislike first, so I won't procrastinate in completing them.
3. Keeping my energy level high by eating a healthy diet and getting enough sleep and exercise.
4. Talking to God about how my priorities match up with His plans for me.
5. Taking time to pray and ask for my parents' advice before making any major plans.

MANNING THE LIFE BOAT

A balanced life is not a self-centered life. It's a life that takes time to reach out to God and others. When you encounter a situation in which someone needs help, whether the person is a friend or a stranger, view it as an opportunity to show love rather than an interruption in your busy day. Ask God if this is a time when you should push the pause button on your own plans and help out.

SAIL ON IN PRAYER

Lord,
Help me understand what a balanced life
looks like. Then help me live one.
I want both my words and the way I live my life
to make You smile. Show me when to say "yes"
and when to say "no." Help me to make time
for the things that matter most.
Amen.

BEING REAL

PURE WATERS

You desire honesty from the womb, teaching me wisdom even there.

Psalm 51:6 NLT

Imagine this: An angel of God appears in your room one night, offering you a complete life makeover. All the physical traits you don't like? Gone—and replaced by traits you desire. Then it's on to other stuff, beyond your face and body. You want a million dollars? Your bank account just got a million bucks fatter. A great car, expensive clothes, all the new electronics—you've got 'em.

What would your new life be like? Your friends would want to be you. Everyone would love you, right? Maybe. Just not the real you. They would be adoring a mirage.

God, the wise and loving Creator of the universe, put you on earth for a purpose—the real you, not the fantasy you. When you let this truth be the source of your identity—instead of muddying the waters with negative feelings about your body or your hair or how much money you have—it gives you power and purpose. It doesn't mean you can't apply some benzoyl peroxide to that pesky acne or try to shed those extra pounds, but that isn't the stuff that defines who you are, the stuff that drives your life. The great painter Pablo Picasso didn't freak out when he started going bald. He just kept on painting masterpieces that museums worldwide fight over and private art collectors pay millions of dollars for.

Like Picasso, you are fully capable of making your unique mark on the world. Don't settle for anything less than the *real* you!

CATCHING THE WAVE

Recently a young Hollywood celebrity made national news by undergoing ten painful, complicated plastic surgery procedures in one day. This attractive woman already had fame, love, and money. But she was still uncomfortable with who she was—especially how she looked.

If only someone had told this insecure young woman that hiding behind a manufactured façade doesn't really gain you anything. It doesn't make people respect or love you more. If you really want closer connections with the people in your life, be real. The person you truly are is more interesting and lovable than anyone you might pretend to be.

SURFING FOR WISDOM

We are God's workmanship, created in Christ Jesus to do good works, which God prepared in advance for us to do.
Ephesians 2:10

You created my inmost being; you knit me together in my mother's womb. I praise you because I am fearfully and wonderfully made; your works are wonderful, I know that full well.
Psalm 139:13–14

Do you not know that your body is a temple of the Holy Spirit, who is in you, whom you have received from God? You are not your own; you were bought with a price. Therefore honor God with your body.
I Corinthians 6:19–20

I have learned the secret of being content in any and every situation.
Philippians 4:12

DIVING FOR UNDERSTANDING

Always be a first-rate version of yourself, instead of a second-rate version of somebody else.
Judy Garland

We are so accustomed to disguise ourselves to others that in the end we become disguised to ourselves.
François de La Rochefoucauld

It takes courage to grow up and become who you really are.
E. E. Cummings

LIFE SAVER CHALLENGE

I will strive to be the real me, not a fake version, by:

1. Sharing my honest opinions and feelings, not what I think people want to hear.

2. Trying to look like the best version of myself, not like some celebrity or popular classmate.

3. Thanking God every day for my unique talents, personal qualities, and insights.

4. Being humble enough to deal with my flaws wisely, not hide them or deny their existence.

5. Making authenticity contagious, as I strive to accept others for who they are, in the same way I want them to accept me.

MANNING THE LIFE BOAT

If you want to share Jesus with the people around you, you can open a lot of doors by simply showing people you are comfortable in your own skin—flaws and all. If you drop your guard, you show someone it's safe to do the same. Sure, if you admit you're imperfect, you can't play the role of all-wise, all-knowing guru, but people don't really need a guru these days. They need a friend.

A *real* friend.

SAIL ON IN PRAYER

Dear loving Creator,
Thank You for creating me,
a unique person in the entire world,
and loving me personally. I'm sorry that I
sometimes go around putting on an act to impress
people or to hide my flaws. May I sense Your love
and acceptance every day. May they inspire me to
live an authentic life. Yes, I'm a work in
progress—that's for sure.
But I'm Your work in progress.
Amen,
and thank You!

BETRAYAL
MAN OVERBOARD!

Bear with each other and forgive whatever grievances you may have against one another. Forgive as the Lord forgave you.

Colossians 3:13

Jake and Nick had been best friends since the eighth grade. They played the same video games, liked the same music, and laughed at the same animated TV shows. They were comfortable at each other's houses and thought of themselves as brothers. Their friends used to joke that they were actually the same person! All this changed at the end of senior year.

Jake's girlfriend of four years, Jessica, broke up with him. Although not completely unexpected—they'd been lukewarm for a while—the reason stunned Jake.

"I like Nick," Jessica said.

Suddenly certain things made sense. The late-night studying at Nick's house, the guitar lessons Nick gave her, and the beach nights that seemed to happen only when Jake was working. Ironically the thought of losing his best friend hurt more than losing his girlfriend. There was a code, unspoken but clear. You don't mess with a friend's girl. But there was another code, just as powerful. Don't let a girl come between you and your best bro.

Betrayal hurts—even when it isn't intentional and things just happen, but definitely when it is purposeful. It takes time to get over a betrayal. Don't let anyone rush you. For your own sake, you will need to forgive, but only you can decide whether to trust that person again. Forgiveness doesn't always mean putting your heart on the line again for someone who has hurt you. Ask, and God will give you the wisdom you need to take the next step.

CATCHING THE WAVE

Betrayal is difficult to deal with because it goes deep, right to the heart. Jesus Himself was betrayed by one of His closest friends, one of His chosen disciples! He certainly knows how it feels. And yet, His instruction is to forgive, even if the betrayer never shows remorse or asks to be forgiven. When you are able to give the hurt to God, the wound can begin to heal. It isn't necessary to tell your betrayer. Just tell God, knowing that He will deal with those who have hurt you, in His way and in His time.

SURFING FOR WISDOM

The LORD longs to be gracious to you;
he rises to show you compassion.
For the LORD is a God of justice. Blessed
are all who wait for him!
Isaiah 30:18

One who forgives an affront fosters
friendship, but one who dwells on disputes
will alienate a friend.
Proverbs 17:9 NRSV

While he was still speaking a crowd came up,
and the man who was called Judas, one of
the Twelve, was leading them.
He approached Jesus to kiss him, but Jesus
asked him, "Judas, are you betraying
the Son of Man with a kiss?"
Luke 22:47-48

Even my close friend, whom I trusted,
he who shared my bread, has lifted up his
heel against me.
Psalm 41:9

LIFE SAVER STORY

Emily knows what betrayal feels like. She sent us this story.

"Recently my boyfriend broke up with me only to date another girl he met. When I found out about it, I was completely devastated; I felt like I had nothing to live for. During this time, I had thoughts of suicide because I was so depressed. The thing that got me through was one of my friends showed me that there is more to this life than what the world has to offer. When someone betrays you, you feel like you're all alone in your troubles. Because of my friend, I can see that I'm not alone. There are many people willing to help others. Maybe I can help someone who has suffered like me."

Have you or someone you love suffered the pain of betrayal? What is your story?

_____

_____

_____

_____

_____

_____

_____

_____

_____

_____

WHAT IT ALL MEANS

be·tray: v. (bē trā)

To break faith with; fail to meet the hopes of; to lead astray; deceive; to share confidential information.

3 THINGS BETRAYAL CAN'T CHANGE

1. Who you are as a person.

2. God's love for you.

3. The purpose God has established for your life.

DIVING FOR UNDERSTANDING

Friends can betray you. Strangers can't.
William C. Dietz

To laugh often and much; to win the respect of intelligent people and the affection of children; to earn the approbation of honest critics and endure the betrayal of false friends ... this is to have succeeded.
Ralph Waldo Emerson

Betrayal can only happen if you love.
John le Carré

LIFE SAVER CHALLENGE

Has someone betrayed you? Try these steps to find the peace that is promised to you:

1. Ask God to help you forgive the one who has hurt you.

2. Confide in a parent or someone you trust about your decision to forgive.

3. Ask God to heal your broken heart.

4. Believe in the peace that is promised to you by God.

MANNING THE LIFE BOAT

Whether your situation involves a friend who carelessly talked about you behind your back, a special someone who now prefers someone else, or a betrayal of another kind, ask God to help you to forgive the one who betrayed you. List the name or names below and pray for each individual.

1.

2.

—— **SAIL ON IN PRAYER** ——

**Father God,
My heart is broken into a million pieces,
and I don't know where to turn. I've been wronged,
and I don't know whom to trust. Help me to know
Your peace and trust You with my fragile heart.
I'm learning that forgiveness is sometimes the only
option. Give me the strength to deal
with betrayal in a way that will bring peace
to my broken heart.
Amen.**

CHANGE
NAVIGATING THE UNFAMILIAR

It is God who works in you to will and to act according to his good purpose.
Philippians 2:13

Sixth grade seemed to run smoothly for Monique. But seventh grade changed everything. She started breaking out in zits at the same time she started noticing boys. Talk about bad timing! Lisa, her "best-best" friend, decided she wanted to hang out with the popular kids, leaving Monique feeling alone and abandoned. Her emotions took her on a roller-coaster ride: up and then down, with increasing intensity. Monique just wanted things to go back to the way they were before, the way they had always been.

You may be feeling the same way—as if the world has done a somersault and left you standing on your head. What you need to understand is that these changes happen for everyone. They are a natural, though often painful, series of changes that will escort you into adulthood. While things will never be the way they were before, at some point life will level out, and you'll be back on your feet. For now, the best plan is to hang on tightly to the loving adults in your life and spend time talking to God about what you're going through. He's always there to listen.

You may not believe it now, but someday you're going to look back on this time in your life and think of it as the fun years. You'll remember the acne and the friendship drama, and you'll smile. You'll see teens struggling with the changes in their lives and you'll want to tell them to hold on, they will survive their teen years just like you did. Really, you will!

CATCHING THE WAVE

The changes you're experiencing right now won't last forever. Whew! Good news, right? But realistically, change will be a permanent part of your life. Your circumstances will change. Your body will continue to change. And when change comes, it's normal to feel some loss of control. There's no better time than now to reach out to God and trust Him to help you navigate the changes ahead. The Bible tells us that He never changes. You can depend on Him to keep you strong and steady no matter what comes your way.

SURFING FOR WISDOM

The Lord cares about our bodies.
1 Corinthians 6:13 NLT

For everything there is a season, a time for every activity under heaven.
Ecclesiastes 3:1 NLT

I trust in you, O LORD; I say, "You are my God." My times are in your hand.
Psalm 31:14-15 NRSV

[God] changes times and seasons; he sets up kings and deposes them. He gives wisdom to the wise and knowledge to the discerning.
Daniel 2:21

LIFE SAVER

DIVING FOR UNDERSTANDING

People told me I shouldn't take everything too seriously, and I didn't listen. Now I wish I had, because I tormented myself over every little thing. What's bad is when you get to age 19, you're looking back thinking, "I wish I could be young again."
Claire Danes

Life is either a daring adventure or nothing. To keep our faces toward change and behave like free spirits in the presence of fate is strength undefeatable.
Helen Keller

Change is the essence of life. Be willing to surrender what you are for what you could become.
Anonymous

LIFE SAVER CHALLENGE

Here's how you can establish patterns in your life that will help you survive this season of change:

1. Remind yourself that God is in control of your life—including the changes you're experiencing right now.

2. Find a healthy outlet to express the jumbled-up emotions that come from the changes. You can do this by talking to a friend, writing in your journal or diary, or confiding in an adult mentor.

3. Talk to God about how you feel. Don't be shy. Tell Him how you really feel.

4. Make sure you talk to a doctor about any unusual changes in your body.

5. If you feel completely overwhelmed, make sure you confide in someone who can help you, like a parent, pastor, counselor, or adult you trust.

MANNING THE LIFE BOAT

As you include God in your life-changing process, you're going to learn some valuable lessons. List two ways you can pass them on to your friends:

1.

2.

SAIL ON IN PRAYER

Dear Jesus,
I may not understand all the changes
that are happening in my life,
but I trust that You are in control.
Please give me patience as I change from
a child into an adult.
Most importantly, change me into the
person You want me to be.
Amen.

COMFORT
CALMING THE STORMY SEA

As a mother comforts her child, so will I comfort you.

Isaiah 66:13

Suppose you're walking home from school. You hear a puppy yelping in fear and pain. You look around for help, but there's no one else nearby. That's when you notice a wriggling ball of black fur trying to free itself from a roll of fencing wire. Instinctively, you try to help. After freeing the entangled pup, you hold it close and try to calm its rapidly beating heart. You whisper gently, "Don't worry. You're going to be okay. I'm here."

If that's how you feel about a puppy, imagine how you'd feel if it was a child who needed help. Your child. God cares for His children as if each one was an only child. Even before you call out to Him, He's there. It's true that you can't feel His arms around you the same way you can a friend's. But that doesn't mean God can't comfort you.

God is near. Always. He knows every detail of what you're going through, as well as the best way to help. The Bible says God keeps every one of your tears in a bottle. Perhaps that bottle even holds the tears you've held tightly in your heart and refused to let fall. No hurt in your life passes unnoticed before your heavenly Father. When you need comfort, turn to Him. As you trust in His promises, He will bring something good out of even the most dire situation. Listen for the gentle whisper of His Spirit that says, "Don't worry. You're going to be okay. I'm here."

CATCHING THE WAVE

Comfort isn't an instant cure for pain or problems. It's more like finding refuge in a storm. Outside, the winds may continue to blow. But you've found a safe place where you can feel free to cry, question, sit in silence, or simply take a deep breath and relax. That safe place is God. He knows you, and the problems you face, inside and out. He also knows what will comfort your hurting heart. Cry out to Him. Then watch to see how His comfort arrives, often in unexpected ways. He will not leave you alone; He will be there for you.

SURFING FOR WISDOM

The LORD is close to the brokenhearted and saves those who are crushed in spirit.
Psalm 34:18

I was very worried, but you comforted me and made me happy.
Psalm 94:19 NCV

You have made me hope.
This is my comfort in my distress, that your promise gives me life.
Psalm 119:49-50 NRSV

Praise be to the God and Father of our Lord Jesus Christ, the Father of compassion and the God of all comfort, who comforts us in all our troubles, so that we can comfort those in any trouble with the comfort we ourselves have received from God.
2 Corinthians 1:3-4

DIVING FOR UNDERSTANDING

You don't have to be alone in your hurt! Comfort is yours.
Joy is an option. And it's all been made possible by your Savior.
Joni Eareckson Tada

God does not comfort us to make us comfortable,
but to make us comforters.
John Henry Jowett

The grace of God is sufficient for all our needs, for every
problem, and for every difficulty, for every broken heart,
and for every human sorrow.
Peter Marshall

LIFE SAVER CHALLENGE

When I'm in need of comfort, I'll remind myself that these five things are true:

1. I'm God's beloved child. (1 John 3:1)

2. God is near. (Psalm 34:18)

3. God can bring good things out of bad. (Romans 8:28)

4. Prayer changes things. (Philippians 4:6–7)

5. God cares about every detail of my life. (Matthew 10:30)

MANNING THE LIFE BOAT

Ask God to bring to mind someone you know who's in need of comfort. List two things you could do to help or encourage that person. Then do them before the week is over.

1.

2.

SAIL ON IN PRAYER

Lord God,
When I'm hurting,
remind me You're near. Comfort me.
Heal me. Help me find real peace.
Make things right and good again.
Show me how to recognize Your hand in
everything. Then, teach me how
I can reach out to help comfort
others when they need it most.
Amen.

COMPASSION
A LOVE FOR THE SEA

Be kind and compassionate to one another, forgiving each other, just as in Christ God forgave you.

Ephesians 4:32

Not everyone will accomplish great things, but anyone can show compassion. Terry wanted to make a difference in people's lives, but his grades weren't great, he didn't have any outstanding talents, and speaking to a group of more than four or five friends made him really nervous.

Dear God, he prayed one night as his eyes welled up with tears. *I want you to use me, but I don't have anything worth using.* He drifted to sleep before the tears dried on his cheeks.

The next day, while sitting at lunch with his friends, he noticed a new kid sitting by himself at a corner table. Terry had never seen him before but, looking at the kid's sad face, he was suddenly overwhelmed with compassion. Before he knew it, Terry was sitting next to the kid, asking him questions, By the end of the day, they had decided to hang out at the mall the next weekend.

That afternoon, while sitting on the school bus going home, Terry realized, *I may not be the most gifted person, but I can love people!* His life was never the same. The next day, Terry began looking for kids to love, kids who no one else noticed, the kind of kids everyone else mistreated. By the end of the school year, Terry had become the silent ringleader of a sizable group of students, some popular and some not-so-popular. Many of them joined him at youth group and decided to follow Jesus.

Who says God can't use certain people? All they need is a little compassion.

CATCHING THE WAVE

Throughout His ministry, Jesus looked upon people with compassion and then healed them. Compassion doesn't mean feeling sorry for someone, it means loving someone who needs help and doing something about it. It means seeing people the way Jesus sees them, and then being available to be used by Jesus to heal them. More lives have been changed through simple acts of compassion than through all the great speakers and gifted personalities in the world. Like Torry realized, anyone can love. If you love Jesus, He can give you the kind of love that can change the world

SURFING FOR WISDOM

The Lord is full of compassion and mercy.
James 5:11

Live in harmony with one another; be sympathetic, love as brothers, be compassionate and humble. Do not repay evil with evil or insult with insult, but with blessing, because to this you were called so that you may inherit a blessing.
1 Peter 3:8–9

As God's chosen people, holy and dearly loved, clothe yourselves with compassion, kindness, humility, gentleness and patience.
Colossians 3:12

This is what the LORD Almighty says: "Administer true justice; show mercy and compassion to one another. ... In your hearts do not think evil of each other."
Zechariah 7:9-10

LIFE SAVER STORY

I was always the kind of person who didn't necessarily "shun" the unpopular kids, but I never reached out to them, either. Less than a year ago, an acquaintance emailed me saying goodbye forever. After pleading with her throughout the evening, she decided not to kill herself that night. Since then, we have become friends. We email for hours about life and the Bible. I have been able to offer her spiritual words of wisdom and remind her that God loves her and cares for her, no matter what she may feel at the time. She has told me multiple times that she is so thankful that she has me to talk to. But I thank her. She helped me realize that reaching out to other kids truly can make a difference, and those small acts of kindness and compassion can save lives and change the world.

Jessica

Have you or someone you love been touched by the compassion of another person? Has someone been touched by your compassion? What is your story?

WHAT IT ALL MEANS

com·pas·sion: noun, kuhm-pash-uhn

A feeling of deep sympathy and sorrow for another who is stricken by misfortune, accompanied by a strong desire to alleviate the suffering.

4 THINGS THAT COMPASSION CAN DO

1. Comfort a hurting heart.

2. Open the door for healing.

3. Affirm that every life has value and purpose.

4. Introduce someone to God's love.

LIFE SAVER

DIVING FOR UNDERSTANDING

By compassion we make others' misery our own, and so,
by relieving them, we relieve ourselves also.
Thomas Browne Sr.

You can't live a perfect day without doing something for someone
who will never be able to repay you.
John Wooden

Too often we underestimate the power of a touch, a smile, a kind
word, a listening ear, an honest compliment, or the smallest act
of caring, all of which have the potential to turn a life around.
Leo Buscaglia

LIFE SAVER CHALLENGE

I commit to living a life of compassion by:

1. Asking Jesus to give me His eyes of compassion.

2. Reading through Matthew, Mark, Luke, and John in my Bible and taking notes on how Jesus touched people with compassion.

3. Writing on a note card, "Anyone can love" and taping it to my bedroom mirror at home or in my locker at school.

4. Looking for kids who are mistreated or overlooked, and reaching out to them.

5. Inviting my friends to join me in changing the world, one person at a time.

MANNING THE LIFE BOAT

Compassion means reaching out to people in need.
Describe a couple of ways you can do this:

1.

2.

SAIL ON IN PRAYER

Dear Jesus,
Please give me Your eyes of compassion,
so I can see people the way You see them
and love people the way You love them.
Grant me the faith to believe that You can
change the world by loving people through me.
Amen.

CONNECTIONS

NO ONE IS AN ISLAND

> **As we have opportunity, let us do good to all people, especially to those who belong to the family of believers.**
>
> *Galatians 6:10*

You could learn a lot from a musk ox. When threatened, these giant hairy residents of the Arctic defend themselves—and their calves—by forming a circle. This formation means that predators like wolves and polar bears will be dealing with the business ends of the oxen's sharp horns—which are sported by both males and females of the species. Alone, a musk ox would be easy prey for a wolf pack or ferocious polar bear, but together, these "bison of the tundra" can ward off their foes.

Togetherness is no less important to humans. Our friends and family offer much more than physical protection. They are our support system in hard times, our advisors when we are confused, our coaches when we need encouragement and motivation.

There is something beautiful and deeply meaningful about worshipping with others, about praying for one another, or learning from one another, challenging each other's assumptions, and sharing real-life stories that demonstrate biblical principles.

Contemporary society honors the rugged individualist, but Jesus challenged those who follow Him to look at themselves as interdependent parts of a human body. Every part has a purpose, and no single part could survive without its connection to the others. It would be like a lone musk ox trying to fight off a wolf pack as it attacked from all sides.

CATCHING THE WAVE

Take a moment or two to consider your close friends and family. Sure, they have their faults. Sometimes they annoy you; other times they are simply predictable and uninteresting. But where would you be without them? Who would you be without them? Think about the time you have invested in those relationships. The adventures you've shared. The laughs. The compliments. The favors.

Being part of a community—a family, a church youth group, or a circle of friends—is vital to life. It's where you draw strength, comfort, and wisdom. And it's a place where you can contribute those very same things.

SURFING FOR WISDOM

Be agreeable, be sympathetic, be loving, be compassionate, be humble. That goes for all of you, no exceptions. No retaliation. No sharp-tongued sarcasm. Instead, bless—that's your job, to bless. You'll be a blessing and also get a blessing.
1 Peter 3:8–9 MSG

It takes wisdom to have a good family, and it takes understanding to make it strong.
Proverbs 24:3 NCV

Love each other like brothers and sisters. Give each other more honor than you want for yourselves.
Romans 12:10 NCV

Behold, how good and how pleasant it is for brethren to dwell together in unity!
Psalm 133:1 KJV

DIVING FOR UNDERSTANDING

We cannot live for ourselves alone. Our lives are connected by a thousand invisible threads, and along these sympathetic fibers, our actions run as causes and return to us as results.
Herman Melville

A good friend is a connection to life—a tie to the past, a road to the future, the key to sanity in a totally insane world.
Lois Wyse

Cherish your human connections—your relationships with friends and family.
Barbara Bush

LIFE SAVER CHALLENGE

I will make human connections a priority in my life by:

1. Becoming active in my church youth group or similar organization.

2. Making sure that technology doesn't become a replacement for real, personal contact.

3. Going to an actual person—not a Web site—when I have a significant problem or question.

4. Spending more time with my family.

5. Praying regularly for my family, friends, and other important people in my life.

MANNING THE LIFE BOAT

Have you ever invited a friend to a church youth event? Youth directors don't continually encourage their charges, "Bring a friend!" just to boost attendance or reduce the amount of leftover pizza they have to deal with. They know that isolation is a danger for all people, but especially for today's teens. It's possible to be digitally connected with hundreds of online presences without being deeply, personally connected to anyone. So, name two friends you could invite to the next youth event.

1.

2.

SAIL ON IN PRAYER

Dear God,
I probably don't thank You enough
for the people in my life.
They are really hard to deal with sometimes,
but when I seriously consider life without them,
I realize how lonely and scary it would be.
Help me to appreciate these people more,
and please give us more quality time together.
I know that I am in their lives,
and they in mine, for a reason.
Amen.

CONTROL & SURRENDER
GO WITH THE FLOW

The plans of the LORD stand firm forever, the purposes of his heart through all generations.

Psalm 33:11

Lauren, at the top of her class, worked hard to submit as many college and scholarship applications as she could during her senior year. She received dozens of teacher recommendations and attached them to well-crafted applications, along with creative and insightful personal essays. She knew the names of the freshman admissions officers at each university. And she knew when to expect a reply announcing her acceptance.

Lauren had planned for college since eighth grade. She maintained a high GPA and got great SAT scores. She logged hundreds of volunteer hours, participated in sports, mastered a musical instrument, learned two foreign languages, and was president of the school's service club. She had it all under control, or so she thought.

The same week acceptance letters started showing up in the mail, Lauren's father lost his job. When he couldn't find work in their area, he moved out of state and mailed his paychecks home. It put a strain on her parents' marriage, and the separation became permanent just weeks before Lauren was to leave for her first-choice college. Lauren decided the timing just wasn't right and stayed home to help her mother with her younger siblings.

It's wise to plan for the future you want. At the same time, you must realize that life can throw you a curve. When that happens, God is there to help you pick up the pieces and rethink your options. After all, He sees the beginning from the end, so He isn't surprised when the river that carries your dreams gets diverted—and He is always ready to help.

CATCHING THE WAVE

Life is a journey. We all think we know where we're going and how to get there. But you may already have learned that things don't always go as planned. When the unexpected happens, you can feel as if your future is spinning out of control. Don't panic! When you place your trust in God, you will always land on your feet. He will help you find a way out, a way over, a way around. Even when your plans fail, God's plans for you never will.

SURFING FOR WISDOM

"I know the plans I have for you," declares the LORD, "plans to prosper you and not to harm you, plans to give you hope and a future."
Jeremiah 29:11

May [the LORD] give you the desire of your heart and make all your plans succeed.
Psalm 20:4

I have learned to be content with whatever I have.
Philippians 4:11 NRSV

Whatever happens, keep thanking God because of Jesus Christ. This is what God wants you to do.
1 Thessalonians 5:18 CEV

DIVING FOR UNDERSTANDING

You can't always control the wind, but you can control your sails.
Anthony Robbins

You cannot control what happens to you, but you can control your attitude toward what happens to you, and in that, you will be mastering change rather than allowing it to master you.
Brian Tracy

Try to control every detail as you seek to achieve your dreams and you will miss the wonderful detours along the way. Leave some room in your plan for sightseeing.
Nadia Grogan

LIFE SAVER CHALLENGE

I will practice surrendering to God by:

1. Making sure that I do control those parts of my life that I can control.

2. Asking God for direction when I feel lost.

3. Calling on my family and friends for wise advice about my situation.

4. Remembering that trusting God is not giving up; it is letting go of my own ideas and letting God show me the way.

MANNING THE LIFE BOAT

Even when you find yourself focused on the busyness of your own life, don't forget about the important people in your life. Sometimes surrendering gives you a chance to reach out to someone else and be their buoy. Name two people in your life that you haven't reached out to in a while:

1.

2.

SAIL ON IN PRAYER

God,
Even when I am busy trying
to keep everything going in my life,
You are there waiting for me just to
let go so You can help.
Thank You for always being present
in my life even when I don't notice.
Help me to learn how to accept those things
I can change and trust You
with all the rest.
Amen.

COURAGE & BOLDNESS

COURAGE IN ROUGH WATERS

[The LORD spoke, saying]: "Be strong and of good courage; do not be afraid, nor be dismayed, for the LORD your God is with you wherever you go."

Joshua 1:9 NKJV

"Hey Brandy, your parents aren't home. Let's go to your place and smoke this joint."

Since third grade, Brandon and his "posse" of friends had hung out together nearly every weekend. They rode their bikes together to the local ice cream shop. On summer nights, they camped in Brandon's backyard and stayed up all night talking about girls and sports. And they laughed all the time. Before moving into middle school, they promised they would always stick together. Seventh grade, however, seemed to change everything. In elementary school, they got into a little bit of trouble, but for the most part, it was harmless fun. But now his "posse" was starting to mess around with girls, doing things he knew they shouldn't do. Then his best friend Nick pulled him aside after school and showed him a joint of marijuana.

"I'm not so sure, Nick. I don't want to get into that stuff," Brandon answered timidly.

"What's wrong with you, Brandon?" Nick looked astonished. "I thought we did everything together. We're best friends! A little weed won't hurt you. What are you, scared?"

It might have been easier for Brandon if he were saying no to someone he barely knew, but this was his friend, his buddy, someone he was close to. It takes a lot of courage to say no to someone you love, someone who's been in your life for a long time. But even though it's more difficult, it's also more important, because what you do can have an impact on what your friend does. Your boldness could keep you both from making mistakes with serious consequences.

CATCHING THE WAVE

It isn't easy to say no. Most teens don't have the courage when pressured to do something they are uncomfortable doing. It takes courage, but you can do it with God's help. When Joshua faced his fears about leading Israel into the Promised Land, God commanded him to be strong and courageous. So what gave Joshua courage? God promised that He would be with him wherever he went. And God's promise includes you, as well. When you need to make unpopular decisions, remember that God is *always* with you, giving you the strength to do the right thing. You are never alone!

SURFING FOR WISDOM

Lord, you are my shield, my wonderful God who gives me courage.
Psalm 3:3 NCV

Wait on the LORD; Be of good courage, and He shall strengthen your heart.
Psalm 27:14 NKJV

When I called, you answered me; you made me bold and stouthearted.
Psalm 138:3

Because the Sovereign LORD helps me, I will not be disgraced. Therefore have I set my face like flint, and I know I will not be put to shame.
Isaiah 50:7

LIFE SAVER

DIVING FOR UNDERSTANDING

Courage is not limited to the battlefield or the Indianapolis 500 or bravely catching a thief in your house. The real tests of courage are much quieter. They are the inner tests, like remaining faithful when nobody's looking, like enduring pain when the room is empty, like standing alone when you're misunderstood.

Charles Swindoll

Courage is what it takes to stand up and speak; courage is also what it takes to sit down and listen.

Winston Churchill

Most of us have far more courage than we ever dreamed we possessed.

Dale Carnegie

LIFE SAVER CHALLENGE

I will grow in courage and boldness by following these three steps:

1. Every morning I will ask God to give me the courage to live for Him.

2. Write a Scripture verse about courage (like Joshua 1:9) on an index card and place it on my bedroom or bathroom mirror.

3. Recruit another friend who loves Jesus and talk on a regular basis about how we can boldly stay away from those things we feel are wrong and find the courage to do the things we feel are right.

MANNING THE LIFE BOAT

Courage can spread like a virus, and you can be the person who infects everyone. Come up with some ideas to start that process:

1.

2.

SAIL ON IN PRAYER

Almighty God,
Please give me the strength
and courage to live the way
You want me to live.
Remind me that Your opinion of me
is more important than the opinion of anyone else.
Most of all, help me remember that
You are always with me.
Amen.

DEPRESSION
KEEPING YOUR HEAD ABOVE WATER

You are my lamp, O LORD; the LORD turns my darkness into light.
2 Samuel 22:29

What do *Harry Potter* author J. K. Rowling, Olympic diver Greg Louganis, astronaut Buzz Aldrin, comedic actor Jim Carrey, and U.S. president Abraham Lincoln have in common? They've all struggled with depression. Could your name be added to that list?

One out of every five teens will struggle with depression before reaching adulthood. If that "one" happens to be you, what do you do? Exactly the opposite of what your emotions tell you to do. You may feel like you want to pull away from people. Hide in your room with your earbuds permanently embedded in your auditory canals. Try to dull the pain with food, video games, alcohol, or drugs. The truth is that all of these options make depression worse, not better.

So where do you turn? A good place to start is in prayer. It's true, God cares about what you do. But He also cares about how you feel. Ask God for the courage to talk to a trusted adult. Tell a relative, teacher, coach, school counselor, or youth pastor what's really going on. Depression isn't a sign of weakness, and many times it's caused by a medical condition that needs attention. A sure sign of strength is reaching out for help when you need it.

If popularity, money, talent, power, or good looks were the secret to never feeling depressed, depression wouldn't have been part of the life stories of the people listed above. If depression is part of your story, don't let it write more than it already has. Reach up to God and out to others for the help you need.

CATCHING THE WAVE

Sadness is usually part of depression. But depression is more than just feeling down. Depression can spark a sudden loss of interest in what you usually enjoy. Strong feelings of grief, shame, hopelessness, and even anger can be warning signs of depression. It's totally normal for you to feel all of these emotions from time to time, especially when facing difficult circumstances. But when strong emotions like these don't seem to let up for more than two weeks straight, don't go it alone. Ask for the help you need to keep your head above water.

SURFING FOR WISDOM

He gives strength to the weary and increases the power of the weak. Even youths grow tired and weary, and young men stumble and fall; but those who hope in the LORD will renew their strength. They will soar on wings like eagles; they will run and not grow weary, they will walk and not be faint.
Isaiah 40:29-31

This is what the LORD Almighty ... says:
"... I will refresh the weary and satisfy the faint."
Jeremiah 31:23, 25

[Jesus said], "Do not let your hearts be troubled. Trust in God; trust also in me."
John 14:1

My soul is downcast within me.
Yet this I call to mind and therefore I have hope: Because of the LORD's great love we are not consumed, for his compassions never fail. They are new every morning; great is your faithfulness.
Lamentations 3:20-23

DIVING FOR UNDERSTANDING

In the depth of winter I finally learned that there was in me an invincible summer.
Albert Camus

Depression loses its power when fresh vision pierces the darkness.
Peter Sinclair

In moments of discouragement, defeat, or even despair, there are always certain things to cling to. Little things usually: remembered laughter, the face of a sleeping child, a tree in the wind—in fact, any reminder of something deeply felt or dearly loved. No man is so poor as not to have many of these small candles. When they are lighted, darkness goes away—and a touch of wonder remains.
"These Small Candles"... tombstone inscription in Britain

LIFE SAVER CHALLENGE

If I feel depressed for more than two weeks, I will:

1. Look at my circumstances and see if there's something I need to change.

2. Ask God for the courage to reach out for help.

3. Speak honestly and openly about my depression to a trusted adult.

4. Immediately talk to an adult or call 1-800-SUICIDE if my thoughts start to focus on hurting myself.

5. Continue to seek help as long as my depression continues, and turn to a counselor or medical professional if things don't get better.

MANNING THE LIFE BOAT

If someone you care about shows signs of depression, or talks about suicide, do the loving thing. Take action. Have an honest conversation. Ask questions. Pray. If your friend or loved one is hesitant to reach out for help, reach out for them. Talk to a trusted adult or call a crisis hotline. The Youth America Hotline at 877-968-8454 has trained teen operators who can answer your questions and help connect you with counselors and crisis centers in your area.

SAIL ON IN PRAYER

Lord God,
I know You care about every detail
of my life. That includes the ups and downs
of my emotions. Please let me know what's normal
and what's not. If depression becomes part
of my story, give me the courage
and honesty I need to share how I'm feeling
with those who can help.
Amen.

DILIGENCE

FIGHTING THE CURRENT

The diligent find freedom in their work.

Proverbs 12:24 MSG

"I speak without exaggeration," inventor Thomas Edison once said, "when I say that I have constructed three thousand different theories in connection with electric light, each one of them reasonable and apparently likely to be true. Yet in two cases only did my experiments prove the truth of my theory."

Think about the quote above, then do the math: Thomas Edison, a renowned scientific genius, developed 2,998 failed theories in order to produce two successful experiments. In fact, the entire story of the light bulb is a tedious tale of repeated trial and failure. Yet, through it all, Edison stayed focused on his goal. With that goal in mind, he watched each experiment attentively and tried to learn something from each mistake, each false start.

Another lesson can be learned from Edison's adventures with electricity: As his various attempts to carbonize a cotton thread and use it as a light-bulb filament failed, Edison realized that he had to combine extraordinary care and patience with his extraordinary diligence. Matching the right thread thickness with the right carbonization technique was painstaking work, and Edison knew that the more intentional he became about his task, the more patience and precision he needed to avoid ruining or misreading the results of his efforts.

So, follow Edison's lead. As you develop and test your own bright ideas, remember and emulate the diligence exemplified by people like Thomas Edison. If you are patient and persistent, even in the face of setbacks, good things will come to light.

CATCHING THE WAVE

Michael Jordan is regarded by many experts as the best basketball player who ever lived. Jordan's raw athletic talent certainly played a large role in his success. But not the leading role. He regularly competed against athletes who could run faster, jump higher, and bench-press more.

In other words, Jordan competed against a lot of naturally gifted athletes. He had many peers in that department. But he had no peer when it came to the diligence he was willing to invest to hone his skills. Diligence is what separates the very good from the truly great.

SURFING FOR WISDOM

Don't lose a minute in building on what you've been given, complementing your basic faith with good character, spiritual understanding, alert discipline, passionate patience, reverent wonder, warm friendliness, and generous love, each dimension fitting into and developing the others.

1 Peter 1:5–7 MSG

Brothers and sisters, I know that I have not yet reached that goal, but there is one thing I always do. Forgetting the past and straining toward what is ahead, I keep trying to reach the goal and get the prize for which God called me through Christ to the life above.

Philippians 3:13–14 NCV

Let us not become weary in doing good, for at the proper time we will reap a harvest if we do not give up.

Galatians 6:9

God will give to each person according to what he has done. To those who by persistence in doing good seek glory, honor, and immortality, he will give eternal life.

Romans 2:6–7

DIVING FOR UNDERSTANDING

Few things are impossible to diligence and skill. Great works are performed not by strength, but by perseverance.
Samuel Johnson

Being forced to work, and forced to do your best, will breed in you temperance and self-control, diligence and strength of will, cheerfulness and content, and a hundred virtues which the idle will never know.
Charles Kingsley

I never could have done what I have done without the habits of punctuality, order, and diligence, without the determination to concentrate myself on one subject at a time.
Charles Dickens

LIFE SAVER CHALLENGE

I will diligently pursue my goals by striving to follow these steps:

1. I will write my goals down—somewhere that will keep them in front of me, whether that's on my iPhone or a piece of paper taped to my bedroom wall.

2. I will share my goals with family, friends, and leaders who will encourage me, hold me accountable, and give me good advice.

3. I will learn something from every single setback I encounter.

4. I will seek the counsel of people pursuing similar goals to mine.

5. I will pray faithfully for patience and courage in achieving my goals

MANNING THE LIFE BOAT

As you pursue your goals, it's likely you will encounter others who have similar aims in mind. As you encourage one another—or even compete with each other—you will get some great opportunities to show how your faith meshes with your life pursuits. You can talk about how your faith has inspired a particular goal in the first place. You can show how praying and following biblical principles helps you stay diligent, even when chasing a goal that is elusive and frustrating.

SAIL ON IN PRAYER

Dear God,
Life can be so frustrating.
I have big goals, but they seem so distant,
so far-fetched. People have laughed at them. Sometimes I am tempted to give up. Help me to be patient.
Help me to be diligent, to keep working, earning small
victories along the way, learning from my mistakes
and setbacks, and moving on. And, of all my life goals,
may knowing You—being close to You and
serving You—be number one.
Amen.

DISAPPOINTMENT

BODY SURFING

[Jesus said:] "Blessed are you who hunger now, for you will be satisfied. Blessed are you who weep now, for you will laugh."

Luke 6:21

Given the choice, Sam would have picked moving in with his best friend over moving midway through his senior year with his father. But he wasn't given that choice. It wasn't his fault that his father couldn't find a job he liked. It wasn't his fault that they had moved three times already during high school. Whoever said you had to like your job in order to make a living? Sam didn't get it. Didn't his father want him to be happy? Sam overheard him on the phone with his grandmother. All he heard his dad say was, "He's just going to have to learn to live with disappointment like the rest of us!"

Really? Why couldn't things go his way for once? How was he going to make it in a new school this late in the year?

People will always disappoint you. In fact, you've probably disappointed a few people in your life along the way too. Trying to avoid disappointment is like trying to avoid the shore when you body surf. You go along riding awesome waves with nothing between you and the surf but your own skin. Sometimes you catch it right and sail smoothly, but other times you catch the edge and end up with a face full of sand. God knows you're going to go out there again tomorrow—and He envelops you like a wetsuit and protects you so you won't get pummeled. Disappointment is inescapable, but it must not stop you from getting in the water.

CATCHING THE WAVE

It would be great if things always turned out the way we wanted them to, but everyone experiences disappointment from time to time. That disappointment might come in the form of a relationship you thought was perfect until he or she broke up with you. It might come from not getting a spot you really wanted on the cheerleading squad or football team or getting a disappointing grade on a test. The thing about disappointment is that you have to learn how to deal with it. You can let it snag you up, or you can smile, take a breath, and go on to the next thing.

SURFING FOR WISDOM

When times are good, be happy; but when times are bad, consider: God has made the one as well as the other.
Ecclesiastes 7:14

[The LORD says:] "Those who hope in me will not be disappointed."
Isaiah 49:23

We are hard-pressed on every side, yet not crushed; we are perplexed, but not in despair; persecuted, but not forsaken; struck down, but not destroyed.
2 Corinthians 4:8-9 NKJV

Do not rejoice over me, O my enemy; when I fall, I shall rise; when I sit in darkness, the LORD will be a light to me.
Micah 7:8 NRSV

DIVING FOR UNDERSTANDING

We must accept finite disappointment, but never lose infinite hope.
Martin Luther King, Jr.

One's best success comes after their greatest disappointments.
Henry Ward Beecher

Our real blessings often appear to us in the shape of pains, losses, and disappointments; but let us have patience and we soon shall see them in their proper figures.
Joseph Addison

LIFE SAVER CHALLENGE

I will not let disappointment trip me up. I will overcome disappointment by:

1. Accepting it as a normal part of life.

2. Confiding in someone who cares about me when disappointment seems to take over.

3. Actively looking for something good in every situation.

4. Thinking about all the good things God has placed in my life.

MANNING THE LIFE BOAT

You are not the only one who gets disappointed. When you reach out to someone else in need of a friend, you can help them see the sunshine on the other side of disappointment. Name two people—family or friends—who could use some optimism today:

1.

2.

──── **SAIL ON IN PRAYER** ────

Lord God,
Forgive me for letting
disappointment control my life.
Help me remember that some doors
close but others swing wide open before me.
That is Your grace and blessing for me.
Open the eyes of my heart to
see the possibilities, Lord!
Amen.

DISCIPLINE
DIVE RIGHT IN!

Buy the truth and do not sell it; get wisdom, discipline and understanding.
Proverbs 23:23

Some kids seem destined to become superstars. Michelle Wie was a golf pro before she turned 16. Jay Greenberg composed five full-length symphonies by the time he was 12. Gregory Smith was nominated for a Nobel Peace Prize for his work as a children's rights activist at age 10. All were born with phenomenal natural abilities. But it takes more than God-given talent to accomplish what they've done. It also takes discipline.

Michelle started playing golf at age 4. Jay began composing at 3. Gregory Smith graduated from college at 13. Practice, study, and hard work all played an important role in their life stories. How big a role will it play in yours?

"Self-discipline" can sound like a bad thing—like a type of punishment you require of yourself because you've done something wrong. But it's really the character trait that comes from doing the right thing over and over again until it becomes a habit. This kind of discipline turns potential into skill, strength, and success. It helps you move from dreaming about who you could be toward actually becoming the person God created you to be.

Research shows it takes 30 to 40 days to establish a new habit. But first you have to choose to make a change. What habits would you like to build into your life? Eating healthier? Talking to God more often? Becoming a better friend by being a better listener? Sinking more free throws? The sooner you begin acting on those good intentions, the sooner a good habit will take root in your life.

CATCHING THE WAVE

Decide to make a positive change, add a bit of self-discipline, and a good habit is ready to take root. Bad habits, however, seem to slide right into your life without any effort at all. They're a non-choice, a refusal to set limits, a sign that your life is out of control. It's true that God is ultimately in control of this world. But there are things He's given you control over, such as taking care of your own body or choosing how to use your talents and intelligence. Doing your best to care for what's in your control and trusting God to take care of the rest are signs of a disciplined life.

SURFING FOR WISDOM

Discipline isn't much fun. It always feels like it's going against the grain. Later, of course, it pays off handsomely, for it's the well-trained who find themselves mature in their relationship with God.
Hebrews 12:11 MSG

He who heeds discipline shows the way to life, but whoever ignores correction leads others astray.
Proverbs 10:17

God did not give us a spirit of timidity, but a spirit of power, of love and of self-discipline.
2 Timothy 1:7

DIVING FOR UNDERSTANDING

Discipline is the bridge between goals and accomplishment.
Jim Rohn

No life ever grows great until it is focused, dedicated, disciplined.
Harry Emerson Fosdick

The best way to break a bad habit is to drop it.
Leo Aikman

LIFE SAVER CHALLENGE

I will begin a new, positive habit with these five steps:

1. Write down a measurable goal; for example, run one mile each weekday.

2. Ask someone to hold me accountable to my goal.

3. Put a check mark on the calendar each time I achieve my goal.

4. Stick to my goal for 30 days.

5. After 30 days, choose one new positive habit to work on while maintaining the one I've already established.

MANNING THE LIFE BOAT

Building a good habit into your life is much easier with the help of a friend. Ask someone to hold you accountable to your goal. Explain how often you'd like him or her to ask how you're doing. (Don't get angry with that person if you're the one who starts slacking off!) Return the favor by asking if there's a good habit you can help your friend get started on.

— SAIL ON IN PRAYER —

Lord God,
I know building good habits
into my life is important.
But I also know myself. I know that sometimes
"work" and "discipline" are two words
I really don't want to hear.
Every morning, remind me that You're near.
Give me the strength—and discipline—I need
to do the right thing.
Amen.

DOING THE RIGHT THING
IN SEARCH OF CLEAR WATER

Even if you suffer for doing what is right, God will reward you for it. So don't worry or be afraid.
1 Peter 3:14 NLT

Sandy Koufax was the greatest baseball pitcher of his era—maybe of any era. Teammates admired him; opposing batters feared him and his blazing fastball.

So one can only imagine his teammates' dismay—and opponents' glee—as the 1965 World Series began, and Koufax announced he wouldn't play in Game 1.

Koufax's team, the Los Angeles Dodgers, seeing world-championship hopes evaporating, begged Koufax to reconsider, but he wouldn't budge. The game conflicted with Yom Kippur, the holiest day of the year for Jewish believers like Koufax.

Koufax stood firm, and the Dodgers lost the opening game in a blowout. Koufax pitched game 2, but the Dodgers lost again. The devout Koufax came back to pitch well in game 5, with a four-hit shutout. One game later, with the series tied 3–3, Koufax, on very short rest, served up another shutout, and the Dodgers captured the series from the Minnesota Twins.

Doing the right thing is always worth it.

Sometimes taking the high road brings a tangible reward of some kind. Other times it doesn't, at least in this life. Koufax's Yom Kippur sacrifice could have cost his team dearly, but he made it clear that he would honor his faith above his career. He demonstrated that honoring your convictions is a sign of character, and a person of character is more honored in God's eyes than the greatest athlete in the world. Are you living for this kind of honor?

CATCHING THE WAVE

We are all going somewhere—even those of us who feel absolutely stuck. But in reality, we are moving closer to God, willfully moving away from Him, or passively drifting away.

If you're not buying that last sentence, consider this: One person can defiantly refuse to exercise and eat a healthful diet. Another can intend to be healthy but lack the willpower to avoid eating whatever junk food happens to be handy. Both will suffer. Intentions have little to do with outcome. It's what you do, or don't do, that counts. Similarly, doing right involves consistently making deliberate choices to stay on the path God wants you to follow.

SURFING FOR WISDOM

All a man's ways seem right to him, but the LORD weighs the heart. To do what is right and just is more acceptable to the LORD than sacrifice.
Proverbs 21:2–3

Are there those among you who are truly wise and understanding? Then they should show it by living right and doing good things with a gentleness that comes from wisdom.
James 3:13 NCV

He guides the humble in what is right and teaches them his way.
Psalm 25:9

The LORD is my shepherd, I shall not want. He makes me lie down in green pastures; he leads me beside still waters; he restores my soul. He leads me in right paths for his name's sake.
Psalm 23:1–3 NRSV

LIFE SAVER STORY

This is Kimberly's story:

"In school I was the girl who tried to get along with everyone because I always knew how it felt to be picked on all the time. In my junior year of high school, we had a clique in gym class. We heard this new girl was gonna be joining our class and people were making fun of her because she used to go to our school in elementary. Instead of joining with everyone's mockery, we let her join our clique. If not, she would've been left alone. Turns out she was a pretty amazing person. We have all become good friends."

Can you recall a time when you were called upon to do the right thing? Was it difficult for you? How did your friends react? *What is your story?*

_____

_____

_____

_____

_____

_____

_____

_____

_____

_____

WHAT IT ALL MEANS

doing the right thing: jargon

That which is "compellingly" the correct or appropriate thing to use, do, say, etc.; doing what is morally responsible, regardless of consequences.

4 THINGS DOING THE RIGHT THING SAYS ABOUT YOU

1. You have learned to think for yourself.

2. You have courage.

3. You have a good sense of right and wrong.

1. You have the instincts of a good leader.

LIFE SAVER

DIVING FOR UNDERSTANDING

Character is doing the right thing when nobody's looking. There are too many people who think that the only thing that's right is to get by, and the only thing that's wrong is to get caught.
J. C. Watts

Every time I've done something that doesn't feel right, it's ended up not being right.
Mario Cuomo

Have the courage to say no. Have the courage to face the truth. Do the right thing because it is right. These are the magic keys to living your life with integrity.
W. Clement Stone

LIFE SAVER CHALLENGE

In matters big and small, I will do the right thing, remembering that:

1. There are no shortcuts in life. Compromise always comes back to bite you somehow (and somewhere).

2. Precious few things in life feel as good as a clear conscience.

3. God loves me, and His rules are meant to give me the best life possible.

4. No one is above the rules.

5. When I am tempted, I will ask God to help me do the right thing—or run away from the *wrong* thing.

MANNING THE LIFE BOAT

There is nothing wrong with talking about your faith. But talk is cheap. It's the people whose faith guides their choices who make those around them think positively about having a relationship with God. What are some ways you can demonstrate your faith?

1.

2.

SAIL ON IN PRAYER

Dear God,
I keep hearing how important it is
to make the right choices.
I want to do that but sometimes
it's really hard, especially when my friends
don't agree with what I'm doing.
Please help me make the right choices in my life,
even when it doesn't feel very comfortable.
Amen.

ENCOURAGEMENT

BUBBLING BROOKS

Worry weighs us down;
a cheerful word picks us up.

Proverbs 12:25 MSG

Trevor usually cracked jokes whenever he had the chance. But for the last week or so, he'd seemed awfully quiet. Usually he just stared at the floor.

"Trevor, what's going on? You just haven't been yourself for a while," Sarah asked him while they were walking to class.

"I don't know," Trevor answered reluctantly. "I'm having problems keeping up in math. My grades are tanking, and my parents grounded me until my grades get better. I'm just stupid."

"Trevor," Sarah began, "you listen to me. You are not stupid. You're a lot smarter than you think."

By the time they reached their next class, Sarah had rattled off a short list of examples from other classes that proved Trevor was definitely not stupid.

"Your only problem is that you wait until the last minute to finish your homework or study for your tests. You can fix that."

"Thanks," Trevor responded.

Everybody needs a little encouragement. Like a bowl of hot soup on a cold winter's day, encouragement not only warms a person up on the inside, but it also acts like food for the soul. Not everyone can be a great athlete or musician, and not everyone can get straight A's—but anyone can be an encourager. Being an encourager doesn't involve telling people something that isn't true. It means reminding people of what's true about them—something they may have forgotten. Best of all, it's a way God can use you to make a difference in other people's lives.

CATCHING THE WAVE

The word "encourage" in the New Testament means "to come alongside"— like putting your arm around a friend who feels down. The same word is also used to describe the Holy Spirit. God gave the Holy Spirit to "come alongside" us so we wouldn't feel alone or discouraged. When you encourage people, you become a partner with the Holy Spirit in helping people feel better about themselves. When you're feeling down, hang out with people who like to encourage. When they make you feel better about yourself, that's really the Holy Spirit working through them to touch you.

SURFING FOR WISDOM

Encourage one another daily, as long as it is called Today.
Hebrews 3:13

We should keep on encouraging each other to be thoughtful and to do helpful things.
Hebrews 10:24 CEV

If your gift is to encourage others, be encouraging.
Romans 12:8 NLT

Encourage the timid, help the weak, be patient with everyone.
1 Thessalonians 5:14

May our Lord Jesus Christ himself and God our Father encourage you and strengthen you in every good thing you do and say. God loved us, and through his grace he gave us a good hope and encouragement that continues forever.
2 Thessalonians 2:16-17 NCV

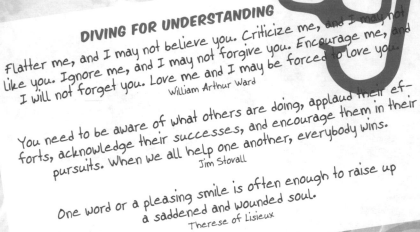

DIVING FOR UNDERSTANDING

Flatter me, and I may not believe you. Criticize me, and I may not like you. Ignore me, and I may not forgive you. Encourage me, and I will not forget you. Love me and I may be forced to love you.
William Arthur Ward

You need to be aware of what others are doing, applaud their efforts, acknowledge their successes, and encourage them in their pursuits. When we all help one another, everybody wins.
Jim Stovall

One word or a pleasing smile is often enough to raise up a saddened and wounded soul.
Therese of Lisieux

LIFE SAVER CHALLENGE

I will make encouragement a bigger part of my life by following these four steps:

1. Keeping a box in my room to store any encouraging cards or notes that people give me.

2. E-mailing an encouraging message to one person each day.

3. Saying something encouraging to at least three people every week.

4. Thinking up creative ways to encourage people—and then doing them!

MANNING THE LIFE BOAT

God wants to encourage people through you.
Name two ways you can come alongside others.

1.

2.

SAIL ON IN PRAYER

God,
Thank You for sending the Holy Spirit
into my life to come alongside me when I feel
discouraged. Help me recognize the people in my
life who will comfort and encourage me.
In the same way, use me to comfort and
encourage the people who need a touch from You.
Amen.

ENTERTAINMENT
SEA OF TRANQUILITY

Let all things be done decently and in order.
1 Corinthians 14:40 NKJV

"Dude, buds out!" Jon jolted Alex out of his heavy metal haze just in time to avoid the assistant principal.

"Man, who cares if we listen to music between classes?" Alex asked, not really expecting an answer, just agreement.

"I've already gotten two referrals on this. Not real interested in getting another," Jon said.

"Whatever. I don't care," said Alex.

"You don't care about much these days," Jon said. "Whatever you're listening to is even louder than us."

Later, at home, Alex's mother said something that seemed important, but Alex didn't respond. After several attempts, she yanked out his ear buds—and pulled him out of his private world. "Are you even here?" she said. "Do you even know you have a family and that things happen that you need to be a part of?"

God loves music. In fact, the Bible is full of songs (psalms) and depictions of His people singing and dancing in praise and worship of Him. It didn't matter what Alex was listening to. Even if he was addicted to Christian music, blocking out the rest of his world in favor of what he heard or what he saw was the problem. God is not like an annoying cymbal; if you listen to what He has to say, it will be music to your ears.

CATCHING THE WAVE

The world is full of noise we call entertainment—computer, video games, music, social networks, movies, and television. Even reading, if it completely consumes you, becomes meaningless if you don't find ways to include others in your enjoyment. Personal entertainment isn't wrong unless it becomes more important than the people and relationships in your life. God's voice can be difficult to hear through all the noise. Enjoy those things that entertain you, but don't let anything own you. Set reasonable limits, and your parents and teachers won't have to.

SURFING FOR WISDOM

I want you to do whatever will help you serve the Lord best, with as few distractions as possible.
1 Corinthians 7:35 NLT

Set your minds on things that are above, not on things that are on earth, for you have died, and your life is hidden with Christ in God.
Colossians 3:2-3 NRSV

We should live in this evil world with wisdom, righteousness, and devotion to God.
Titus 2:12 NLT

Let no one despise your youth, but set the believers an example in speech and conduct, in love, in faith, in purity.
1 Timothy 4:12 NRSV

LIFE SAVER

DIVING FOR UNDERSTANDING

Tell me to what you pay attention, and I'll tell you who you are.
Jose Ortega y Gasset

The main thing is to keep the main thing the main thing.
Stephen Covey

Imagine you are the only real person in a world filled with virtual people on a computer screen. Now think about it. Would you really want to live there?
Judy Fornot

LIFE SAVER CHALLENGE

I will turn down the volume on the entertainment in my life by:

1. Evaluating how much of my time I spend on entertainment, especially with MP3s and games.

2. Increasing the time I spend interacting with others.

3. Reaching out to those in my close circle in meaningful ways.

4. Finding time every day to listen to God.

MANNING THE LIFE BOAT

Personal entertainment is just that—personal. How can you widen the circle of your enjoyment by including others? Name two things you now do by yourself that you could do with others instead:

1.

2.

SAIL ON IN PRAYER

Heavenly Father,
Help me know when I'm out of balance
and spending too much time in my own world.
Show me how I can enjoy music and games
without letting them take over my life.
Amen.

FAITH
SURFING DESPITE ALL ODDS

Faith is being sure of what we hope for and certain of what we do not see.
Hebrews 11:1

People often say, "Seeing is believing." But faith says, "There's more to life than what you can see with your eyes." Faith is a way of believing that opens you up to a new way of seeing. You can't see God. He's Spirit, not flesh. But as you get to know Him through prayer and reading the Bible, you begin to see yourself, others, and life in a brand-new light.

Just ask Bethany Hamilton. On her website (BethanyHamilton.com), Bethany writes, "No matter who you are, God can use you … You might think, 'Why would God use me?' (That's what I thought. I was like 13, and there God goes using me!)" The way God has used Bethany to inspire others is something many would see as a tragedy. But through faith, Bethany has a new outlook on life.

In 2003, thirteen-year-old Bethany was surfing near her home in Hawaii when a shark severed her left arm. After paddling 20 minutes to shore, Bethany almost died from blood loss. But after several surgeries and lots of support from family and friends, Bethany was back in the water in less than a month. A few months later, she was surfing competitively.

Before she lost her arm, Bethany had prayed God would use her. Today, God continues to answer that prayer. Bethany's still surfing competitively. She's written books, appeared on *Oprah* and is currently working on a movie about her life—and her faith. Bethany admits life isn't easy, but she's seen firsthand how faith in God can change tragedy into something wonderful and unexpected.

CATCHING THE WAVE

Everyone puts his or her faith in something. Some people trust in money. Some put their confidence in science. Others believe if you live a good life, good things will happen to you. But just because you believe in something doesn't make it true. In the Bible, Jesus refers to Himself as "the way, the truth, and the life." If you're looking for guidance, for what is real, for a life that matters, and hope that lasts beyond this world and into the next, put your faith in Jesus. You can trust that His love and power will never fail.

SURFING FOR WISDOM

We live by faith, not by sight.
2 Corinthians 5:7

As you therefore have received
Christ Jesus the Lord,
continue to live your lives in him,
rooted and built up in him and established
in the faith, just as you were taught,
abounding in thanksgiving.
Colossians 2:6-7 NRSV

For by grace you have been saved
through faith, and this is not your own
doing; it is the gift of God—not the result
of works, so that no one may boast.
Ephesians 2:8-9 NRSV

Take up the shield of faith, with which
you can extinguish all the flaming arrows
of the evil one.
Ephesians 6:16

Let us draw near to God with a sincere heart
in full assurance of faith
Hebrews 10:22

DIVING FOR UNDERSTANDING

Faith isn't the ability to believe long and far into the misty future. It's simply taking God at His Word and taking the next step.
Joni Eareckson Tada

Faith is putting all your eggs in God's basket, then counting your blessings before they hatch.
Ramona C. Carroll

Faith is daring the soul to go beyond what the eyes can see.
William Newton Clarke

LIFE SAVER CHALLENGE

When I struggle with doubt, I will take action with these five steps:

1. Turn toward God, instead of away from Him.

2. Honestly tell God how I feel.

3. Accept that God is too big for me to ever fully understand.

4. Ask God to help me more clearly see Him at work in my life.

5. Act on whatever I believe God is asking me to do.

MANNING THE LIFE BOAT

Sharing your faith simply means sharing the story of what God is doing in your life. You don't have to have all of the answers. Just be honest about your faith, struggles and all. Ask God to bring one person to mind, then pray for the courage and the right time to share your story with them.

SAIL ON IN PRAYER

Lord God,
It isn't always easy to believe
in someone I can't see.
But I want to believe in You.
I want to trust You with every part of my life.
Teach me how.
Help me see my circumstances through Your eyes.
Make my faith grow stronger,
day by day.
Amen.

FAITHFULNESS

AVOIDING "GO WITH THE FLOW"

The faithful will abound with blessings.

Proverbs 28:20 NRSV

Imagine you're being followed. Not in any sinister way. Imagine that you've asked someone to follow you and carefully record how you spend your free time.

You might be surprised at the results. With most people today, there is a big disconnect between what they claim to value and the stuff that actually occupies their time. For example, lots of people profess a sincere devotion to God. They say they are faithful to Him, and most are sincere when they say it. But in reality, God often gets only an hour of our time on the weekend—and maybe a few hurried prayers in between.

On a similar note, "family" is a stated priority for millions of people, but parents, siblings, and other family often get a pretty small percentage of their time.

It's amazing how many things can subtly steal our time and attention. You-Tube videos can become so addictive that they gobble up hours at a time. Chilling out in front of the TV to watch a favorite show can evolve into three hours of vegging out, remote in hand.

Speaker and author Charles Swindoll is famous for posing this challenge: "Show me where you put most of your time and money, and I'll show you what you truly value in life."

To be truly faithful to God and to the people in our lives, we must make a deliberate choice and take deliberate action—to invest time, thought, and effort. Being faithful doesn't happen by default. And merely wanting to be faithful doesn't make us so—any more than wanting to be smart will add points to an IQ score.

CATCHING THE WAVE

Consider this: You can train for a marathon by investing 15 intense, high-quality minutes of running, stretching, and weight training every day. But even with the world's best running coach and state-of-the art training equipment, that program is not going to carry you for 26.2 miles. It takes regular runs of 20 miles to build the endurance, strength, and mental toughness to get the job done. There are no shortcuts.

A truly meaningful relationship with God and the significant people in your life is like a marathon. You have to be willing to faithfully invest your time if you want to go the distance.

SURFING FOR WISDOM

Let love and faithfulness never leave you; bind them around your neck, write them on the tablet of your heart. Then you will win favor and a good name in the sight of God and man.
Proverbs 3:3-4

The LORD has set apart the faithful for himself; the LORD hears when I call to him.
Psalm 4:3 NRSV

The LORD loves the just and will not forsake his faithful ones.
They will be protected forever.
Psalm 37:28

It is required that those who have been given a trust must prove faithful.
1 Corinthians 4:2

LIFE SAVER

DIVING FOR UNDERSTANDING

I do not pray for success, I ask for faithfulness.
Mother Teresa

Your faithfulness makes you trustworthy to God.
Edwin Louis Cole

If you be faithful, you will have that honor that comes from God: his Spirit will say in your hearts, Well done, good and faithful servants.
Adam Clarke

LIFE SAVER CHALLENGE

I will be more faithful to God and to others by:

1. Giving some thought to my free time and getting an accurate picture of whether the way I spend my days matches what I claim to value.

2. Making my relationship with God part of my regular routine—through daily devotions, daily prayer, and regular Bible reading.

3. Setting limits on things that tend to suck up too much of my time.

4. Being willing to make—and keep—promises and commitments.

5. Seeking help if I sense I have an addiction to or dependence on playing video games, surfing the Web, watching TV, or similar activities.

MANNING THE LIFE BOAT

Even if they don't admit it openly, people admire those who are actually faithful to do what they say they are going to do. And doing what you say you are going to do could open a door for you to talk about commitment to the most important thing in the world.

SAIL ON IN PRAYER

Dear God,
Where did the time go?
How many times have I heard myself wonder this?
There are a lot of subtle time-thieves in my life. Help me to keep my eyes open, to take control of my time.
I want to be faithful to You and to the people You've placed in my life. But want-to isn't enough. Please help me to ensure that my actions match my intentions.
Amen.

FEAR
SURFING THROUGH SHARK-INFESTED WATERS

When I am afraid, I will trust in you.
Psalm 56:3

Noah sat down at his desk and took a deep breath. It was the first day of school after the best summer of his life. But this felt like the first day of his new life. During a mission trip to Mexico with his youth group, he had invited Jesus into his heart and life. The rest of the summer went by like a blur. He couldn't remember ever being so happy and peaceful inside.

But today was different. Living your faith is much easier when your friends at school aren't around. Sitting at his desk, he could feel his forehead and hands start to sweat as fear began gripping him. *Jesus, I'm not sure I can do this*, he prayed under his breath. *Please give me the courage to live for You.*

You may be facing the same fear as Noah. You want to live for Jesus, but you're afraid people will make fun of you for being a Christian or accuse you of thinking you're better than they are.

First of all, know this: You're not alone. Millions of students around the world face the same challenge. While you don't want to turn your back on your friends who don't know Jesus, you'll find strength from hanging out with others who believe the way you do. But most of all, remember that what Jesus thinks about you is more important than what other people think. And He thinks you're awesome!

CATCHING THE WAVE

Everyone wrestles against fear—even great people in the Bible like Abraham and his wife Sarah. Ignoring or denying it won't make it go away, so you're better off admitting it. Sometimes acknowledging your fear is all you need to remove its stranglehold. If fear still bothers you, let it drive you to Jesus. Remember that regardless of what makes you afraid, Jesus is greater. The Bible says that when you call on the name of Jesus, everything in heaven and on earth must bow down to Him. So drawing close to the greatest power in the universe is the best way to overcome your fear.

SURFING FOR WISDOM

Don't be afraid. Just stand still and watch the LORD rescue you.
Exodus 14:13 NLT

Do not fear, for I am with you; do not be dismayed, for I am your God. I will strengthen you and help you; I will uphold you with my righteous right hand.
Isaiah 41:10

[The LORD said:] "Be strong and of good courage; do not be afraid, nor be dismayed, for the LORD your God is with you wherever you go."
Joshua 1:9 NKJV

I sought the LORD, and he answered me; he delivered me from all my fears.
Psalm 34:4

DIVING FOR UNDERSTANDING

FEAR is an acronym in the English language for "False Evidence Appearing Real."
Neale Donald Walsch

You block your dream when you allow your fear to grow bigger than your faith.
Mary Manin Morrissey

There are four ways you can handle fear. You can go over it, under it, or around it. But if you are ever to put fear behind you, you must walk straight through it. Once you put fear behind you, leave it there.
Donna A. Favors

LIFE SAVER CHALLENGE

In order to overcome any fear in my life, I will follow these three steps:

1. List all my fears in a journal and then write down why my fears seem so real.

2. Explain my fears to a friend I trust. If the person loves God the way I do, I'll ask the person to pray for me.

3. Spend time reading and praying over Scripture passages about fear, like 2 Timothy 1:7, 1 Peter 5:8-9, and 1 John 4:18.

MANNING THE LIFE BOAT

No matter what fears trouble you, God can still use you to help others. Name two ways you can help someone you love overcome his or her fear.

1.

2.

—— SAIL ON IN PRAYER ——

Almighty God,
No longer will I allow fear to control me.
Remind me that because I am in Your hands,
You will never leave me nor forsake me.
Open my eyes to see that You are greater than any
problem, any power, or any person.
And because of that, I can trust in You.
Amen.

FOCUS
LOCATOR BEACON

Our only goal is to please God.
2 Corinthians 5:9 NCV

Lindsey's decision to enter the school talent show now felt like a big mistake. What was she thinking? How did she let herself get talked into this? Her friends harassed her for weeks, telling her she had to share her musical talent. Now as she stood behind the curtain, her stomach flipped in protest; her mouth felt full of cotton. What if they didn't like her music? The curtain opened; the main spotlight caught her panic like a prisoner trying to escape. The expectant audience waited in silence. Her fingers fiddled with the guitar strings in an attempt to delay the inevitable. She knew there was a full house, but she couldn't discern any one form beyond the spotlight. It was as if she was alone in the theater.

There was only one person in that audience that Lindsey felt comfortable playing for—her father. She decided that if she focused her performance on him, she could relax. And she did. Her performance was flawless, and the only indication that she wasn't alone came when the roar of applause hit her like a tidal wave. At that moment, the spotlight became her friend and not her captor; it helped her ignore the masses and keep the main thing the main thing.

You may find that you do what you do for the wrong reasons or to please the wrong people. God is the only member of your audience that matters. Focus on pleasing Him, and you will find it easier to consistently do your best in whatever you endeavor and enjoy yourself while you're doing it.

CATCHING THE WAVE

The Bible says you are rewarded when you live your life to please God and not people. It's hard to stay focused on what is most important, but if you intentionally focus your efforts on pleasing God, you may find that you please others as well. A job well done is a job well done, no matter who's watching. When you keep the main thing the main thing, you may realize you're standing a little taller, feeling a little stronger, and feeling less anxious about what comes next. Remember that God is not a feared critic in your audience; He's your biggest fan!

SURFING FOR WISDOM

My eyes are fixed on you, O Sovereign LORD; in you I take refuge.
Psalm 141:8

If you devote your heart to him and stretch out your hands to him ... then you will lift up your face without shame; you will stand firm and without fear.... You will be secure, because there is hope; you will look about you and take your rest in safety.
Job 11:13, 15, 18

Acknowledge the God of your father, and serve him with wholehearted devotion and with a willing mind, for the LORD searches every heart and understands every motive behind the thoughts. If you seek him, he will be found by you; but if you forsake him, he will reject you forever.
1 Chronicles 28:9

Keep your eyes focused on what is right, and look straight ahead to what is good. Be careful what you do, and always do what is right.
Proverbs 4:25-26 NCV

DIVING FOR UNDERSTANDING

Focused, hard work is the real key to success.
Keep your eyes on the goal, and just keep
taking the next step towards completing it.
John Carmack

The sun's energy warms the world.
But when you focus it through a magnifying glass
it can start a fire.
Focus is so powerful!
Alan Pariser

Without goals, you will end up going nowhere or you will end up
following someone else's map! Develop your map today—set
your goals and focus!
Catherine Pulsifer

LIFE SAVER CHALLENGE

I will try to focus my efforts on pleasing God by:

1. Beginning each day by asking God to choose my path for me.

2. Being faithful with the responsibilities given to me.

3. Asking someone I trust to let me know if I start acting like it's all about me.

4. Remembering that God is not waiting to judge me but is waiting to pat me on the back and say, "Well done!"

MANNING THE LIFE BOAT

Name two things you can do to please God that will also be pleasing to others:

1.

2.

SAIL ON IN PRAYER

Father God,
Thank You for the gifts and talents
You've given me in this life.
Show me how to use them for Your good
pleasure. Help me to stay focused on the path
to pleasing You, so that I might hear
Your rousing applause.
Amen.

FORGIVENESS

SWIMMING IN OPEN WATER

Forgive anyone who does you wrong, just as Christ has forgiven you.

Colossians 3:13 CEV

Imagine being sent to prison for doing the right thing. You're starved and worked to the point of exhaustion. You sleep on a dirty, lice-ridden cot. Five members of your innocent family are imprisoned along with you. Four of them die. When you're finally set free, what's one of the first things you want to do? "Get even" might rise to the top of the list.

A Dutch woman named Corrie ten Boom lived this nightmare firsthand. When she was set free from the Ravensbrück concentration camp after World War II, she held tightly to two things God taught her during her time in the death camp: "There is no pit so deep that God's love is not deeper still" and "God will give us the love to be able to forgive our enemies." That doesn't mean Corrie didn't struggle with feelings of hate or a desire for revenge. But she knew the high price of holding on to these feelings, of feeding them so they'd grow.

Refusing to forgive someone who has hurt you is its own kind of prison. As you feed bitterness and anger by running the tapes of how you've been wronged over and over in your head, you hurt no one but yourself. If you act on your emotions and do or say something as payback, you add guilt to the mix. You wind up as guilty as the one you refuse to forgive. It takes the two truths Corrie learned to truly be set free. Only the power of God's love is strong enough to forgive what seems unforgivable.

CATCHING THE WAVE

Since the beginning of the world, people have turned away from God. They wanted to do things their way, even when they knew God's way was better for them. This caused a break in the relationship between God and His children. This is why Jesus came to earth and gave His life on the cross. Through His sacrifice, we're forgiven. Our relationship with God is mended. When we refuse to forgive those who turn against us, we're refusing to follow Jesus' example. Choosing to love means choosing to let go of anything standing in the way of our relationship with God and others.

SURFING FOR WISDOM

If you forgive anyone, I also forgive him. And what I have forgiven—if there was anything to forgive—I have forgiven in the sight of Christ for your sake.

2 Corinthians 2:10

In [Jesus] we have redemption through his blood, the forgiveness of sins, in accordance with the riches of God's grace.

Ephesians 1:7

[Jesus said,] "Whenever you stand praying, if you have anything against anyone, forgive him, that your Father in heaven may also forgive you your trespasses."

Mark 11:25 NKJV

Peter came to Jesus and asked, "Lord, how many times shall I forgive my brother when he sins against me? Up to seven times?" Jesus answered, "I tell you, not seven times, but seventy-seven times."

Matthew 18:2-22

LIFE SAVER

DIVING FOR UNDERSTANDING

To forgive is to set a prisoner free and discover that the prisoner was you.
Lewis B. Smedes

Always forgive your enemies—nothing annoys them so much.
Oscar Wilde

Forgiveness ought to be like a cancelled note—torn in two and burned up, so that it never can be shown against one.
Henry Ward Beecher

LIFE SAVER CHALLENGE

I will begin to forgive with these five steps:

1. Ask God to show me if there's anyone I'm holding a grudge against.

2. Tell God exactly how I feel I've been wronged.

3. Picture putting each and every grudge in God's hands.

4. Ask God to help me let go of any bitterness I feel.

5. Pray for God's blessings to flow in the lives of my enemies.

MANNING THE LIFE BOAT

Sometimes we need to say the words "I forgive you" to someone who has hurt us. If your "enemy" is sorry for what happened, don't hold back. Say the words he or she needs to hear and you need to say. Then continue to pray for this person, until your hard feelings fade away.

SAIL ON IN PRAYER

Lord God,
Thank You for all of the things You've forgiven in my life. Help me realize how much that forgiveness cost Jesus. Then, please help me forgive those who hurt me. Even if my feelings don't match up to my words right away, help me continue to forgive until Your love breaks through.
Amen

FRIENDSHIP

FISHING FOR FRIENDS

The righteous should choose his friends carefully, for the way of the wicked leads them astray.
Proverbs 12:26 NKJV

"So what happened to you?" Sonja's mother asked her. "Over the last month you've started making some very poor choices. First, you stopped coming home right after school, and you won't tell us where you've been. And now you've been caught shoplifting. I just don't understand."

The two looked at each other for a moment before Sonja explained, "I didn't have any friends until Shelby asked me to hang out with her and Kayla. They get in trouble sometimes ... but at least they like me."

People become friends for many reasons—loneliness, acceptance, mutual interests, mutual problems, shared classes, and church affiliation, to name just a few. Most people would say they didn't choose their friends at all; they just ended up together. But the Bible tells us that we can and should intentionally choose our friends. That doesn't mean you should shun people you think aren't good enough for you. What it does mean is that you are wise in regard to friendship. You don't spend time with people who regularly ask you to do things you know are wrong. You don't spend time with people who treat you disrespectfully or abusively. You don't spend time with people who mistreat others.

If you need a friend, ask God to point out to you those people who bring out the best in you. Look for acts of kindness and compassion. Listen for those voices that are not putting others down. When you find someone like that—reach out! That person may be looking for a friend just like you.

CATCHING THE WAVE

Friends are important. Choosing the right friends is even more important. So what makes a good friend? The Bible describes the kind of love evident in true friendship as being loving, patient, kind, and never jealous, boastful, proud, rude, or selfish. It always protects the other person, trusts, hopes, and perseveres. You probably won't find someone who exhibits all these qualities, but it will be easy to spot someone who is working in that direction. And working toward these attributes in your own life will draw the right friends to you.

SURFING FOR WISDOM

Two are better than one, because they have a good reward for their toil. For if they fall, one will lift up the other; but woe to one who is alone and falls and does not have another to help.
Ecclesiastes 1:9-10 NRSV

A friend loves at all times, and a brother is born for adversity.
Proverbs 17:17 NKJV

The godly give good advice to their friends.
Proverbs 12:26 NLT

Friends come and friends go, but a true friend sticks by you like family.
Proverbs 18:24 MSG

LIFE SAVER STORY

Kenzie wanted to share this heads-up about friendship:

"If any of you are going through a tough stage, you are not alone. I am going through it too. When I was struggling, I talked to my parents, my really, really close friends, and my youth group. Most importantly, I prayed about my struggles. Every day, before I go to school, me and my mom pray that I can get through the day. When you are hanging out with your friends, don't hang out with the ones that influence you to do the wrong kind of things. If you are not part of a youth group, you should join because it will influence you to do good things. I really hope this story will help you and make your life easier."

Has something happened in your life that demonstrated the true meaning of friendship? What is your story?

_____

_____

_____

_____

_____

_____

_____

_____

_____

WHAT IT ALL MEANS

friend·ship: n., (frĕnd shĭp)

The quality or condition of being friends; a friendly relationship; friendliness and good will.

4 QUALITIES OF TRUE FRIENDSHIP

1. Loyalty (A true friend will stay by you in the good times and in the bad times.)

2. Honesty (A true friend will tell you what you need to hear—not just what you want to hear.)

3. Generosity (A true friend will share what he or she has with you.)

4. Love (A true friend loves you—the real you—just the way you are.)

LIFE SAVER

DIVING FOR UNDERSTANDING

Blessed are they who have the gift of making friends, for it is one of God's best gifts. It involves many things, but above all, the power of going out of one's self and appreciating whatever is noble and loving in another.
Thomas Hughes

Life is partly what we make it, and partly what it is made by the friends we choose.
Tennessee Williams

Be slow to fall into friendship; but when thou art in, continue firm and constant.
Socrates

LIFE SAVER CHALLENGE

The best way to build a good friendship is to be a good friend. Here are a few ways to become a good friend:

1. Show sincere interest in the things that interest your friend.

2. Be a good listener.

3. Stand up for your friend; don't allow anyone to talk badly about that person in your presence.

4. Treat your friend with respect.

5. Invite your friend into your walk with God by going to church or youth group together—or even praying for one other.

MANNING THE LIFE BOAT

You need friends—and so do other people. If you know of someone who doesn't appear to have any friends, why not make that person your friend? List some ways you can befriend someone you don't already know.

1.

2.

SAIL ON IN PRAYER

Dear Jesus,
You're the greatest friend I'll ever have.
Please help me be the kind of friend that
You are to me. Steer me away from the
people who could steer me away from You,
and point me to the people
who will point me to You.
Amen.

GIVING & GENEROSITY

SHARING THE LIFE BOAT

God loves a cheerful giver.

2 Corinthians 9:7 NASB

Zell Kravinsky is a real estate magnate who has a fortune of about $45 million. Or had. Recently Kravinsky donated almost all of his money to various health-related charities. He has a soft spot for those who struggle with health challenges.

If you're not impressed by Kravinsky yet, you will be. He didn't stop at giving away almost all of his money. After learning that thousands of people die each year while waiting for kidney transplants, he contacted a local hospital and invited doctors to cut him open. Then he donated one of his kidneys. To a total stranger.

Kravinsky's story raises an important question: If money and material goods bring happiness, why would a multimillionaire give just about everything away—including an irreplaceable organ from his own body?

What does this guy know that others don't? A few years ago, the authors of the book *Wake Up and Smell the Pizza* conducted in-depth interviews with the happiest, most well-adjusted people they knew. These people represented a wide range of ages, ethnic groups, and income levels, but they all had this in common. They were crazy-generous. They gave presents for no reason. They lent out books, CDs, even their cars. And the giving didn't stop with material things. They gave their time, their talent, and their love. They poured their lives into the lives of others.

This sounds like the opposite of today's "I'm gonna get mine" culture, but giving, not getting, brings true happiness. Think about the greedy people you know. Are they full of joy?

In the Bible, Jesus constantly urged people to give, especially to the needy. That call to generosity still rings true. If you haven't done so already, give *giving* a chance.

CATCHING THE WAVE

If you're like most teens, the idea of giving to the needy might scare you. In your mind, you are one of the needy. Good news: Giving doesn't need to be limited to money. You can donate clothes, your old clarinet, or books you've already read. You can donate your time––at a soup kitchen, rescue mission, or homeless shelter. Some teens serve as peer counselors at their school. Others share their expertise as tutors for adults trying to earn their GED.

The possibilities outnumber the stars in the sky. The important thing is to give *something*. Giving puts your very soul in harmony with Jesus. Try it and see.

SURFING FOR WISDOM

Give freely and spontaneously. Don't have a stingy heart. The way you handle matters like this triggers GOD, your God's, blessing in everything you do, all your work and ventures.
Deuteronomy 15:10 MSG

Whoever gives to the poor will lack nothing.
Proverbs 28:27 NRSV

Those who are generous are blessed.
Proverbs 22:9 NRSV

[Jesus said,] "Give, and it will be given to you. A good measure, pressed down, shaken together and running over, will be poured into your lap. For with the measure you use, it will be measured to you."
Luke 6:38

They gave in a way we did not expect: They first gave themselves to the Lord and to us. This is what God wants.
2 Corinthians 8:5 NCV

DIVING FOR UNDERSTANDING

Giving is a joy if we do it in the right spirit.
It all depends on whether we think of it as
"What can I spare?" or as "What can I share?"
Esther York Burkholder

You do not have to be rich to be generous.
If he has the spirit of true generosity,
a pauper can give like a prince.
Corinne U. Wells

Remember that there is no happiness in having or in getting,
but only in giving. Reach out. Share. Smile. Hug.
Og Mandino

LIFE SAVER CHALLENGE

I will be a more generous person by:

1. Giving a donation to a worthy charity every month—even if that donation is small.

2. Not hanging on to things I don't need or don't need very much.

3. Sharing my talents, time, and energy.

4. Remembering that I'm supposed to control my material possessions—they're not supposed to control me.

5. Going to my pastor, youth pastor, or local youth leader this week and asking, "How can I help?"

MANNING THE LIFE BOAT

If you want to show people in your life who Jesus is and how He has changed your life, a genuine act of giving will go a lot further than any sermon or religious "sales pitch" you can deliver. Generosity touches people deep in the heart, and the heart is the part Jesus is most interested in.

SAIL ON IN PRAYER

Dear God,
Help me to be generous with everything
You have given me. Let me enjoy the pure joy
that comes from letting go of what I have and giving
it to people who need it so much more than I do.
May I remember always that giving makes me
more like You, because
You gave everything for me.
Amen.

GRATITUDE
QUENCHING A THIRST

Be thankful in all circumstances.
1 Thessalonians 5:18 NLT

Jeff and Lyn were required to log 75 volunteer hours in order to qualify for state scholarships for college. They dreaded it, but they both signed up to work with Habitat for Humanity. Disappointed that they were too young to use any power tools, they were relegated to cleaning up the construction site and serving lemonade to the other workers. When the house was finished, they were there to welcome its new owners. Jeff couldn't wait to get signed out so they could get back to their real lives.

"Thank you," a guy about Jeff's age said. "We appreciate you taking the time to help."

"No problem, man," Jeff said. "It was nothing."

Jeff watched as the young man walked into one of the newly painted bedrooms. He unpacked a small duffel bag and carefully hung two T-shirts with their school logo on hangers. "Hey, you play ball for our school, don't you?" asked Jeff. "Those are team shirts, right?"

"Yeah," the other guy said and quickly closed the closet door. "Like I said."

Jeff and Lyn climbed into his Camaro and sped away. "I just didn't know," Lyn said finally.

"What?" said Jeff.

"Those were his only shirts! And he got those from being on the team," Lyn said.

What's nothing to you may be something to someone else. God wants you to give thanks for every *someone* and every *something*.

CATCHING THE WAVE

Every time you give thanks, you give thanks to God. Even when you think you're thanking a friend or family member, God is at the heart of gratitude. The Bible says He has plans to bless and not harm you, so even in the small things you can give thanks. It's easy to take what you have for granted, but the food on your table and the roof you find over your head each night are worthy of thanks. You can be grateful to have a closet to hang two shirts in, and you can be thankful for the chance to build that closet for someone else. Gratitude is an attitude, one that must become a habit.

SURFING FOR WISDOM

Thanks be to God, who gives us the victory through our Lord Jesus Christ.
1 Corinthians 15:57 NRSV

Let the peace of Christ rule in your hearts, to which indeed you were called in the one body. And be thankful.... And whatever you do, in word or deed, do everything in the name of the Lord Jesus, giving thanks to God the Father through him.
Colossians 3:15, 17 NRSV

Thank you! Everything in me says, "Thank you!" Angels listen as I sing my thanks. I kneel in worship facing your holy temple and say it again: "Thank you!" ... Thank you for your faithfulness.
Psalm 138:1-2 MSG

O give thanks to the LORD, for he is good; for his steadfast love endures for ever.
Psalm 107:1 NRSV

I give thanks to God with everything I've got—wherever good people gather, and in the congregation. God's works are so great, worth a lifetime of study—endless enjoyment!
Psalm 111:1-2 MSG

DIVING FOR UNDERSTANDING

Gratefulness is the key to a happy life that we hold in our hands, because if we are not grateful, then no matter how much we have we will not be happy—because we will always want to have something else or something more.

David Steindl-Rast

Let us be grateful to people who make us happy; they are the charming gardeners who make our souls blossom.

Marcel Proust

Feeling gratitude and not expressing it is like wrapping a present and not giving it.

William Arthur Ward

LIFE SAVER CHALLENGE

I will make gratitude a regular habit by:

1. Setting aside a time each day to reflect on what I can be thankful for.

2. Keeping a gratitude journal by writing down five things I'm grateful for every day.

3. Finding something to be thankful for even when I'm feeling disappointed or discouraged.

4. Looking for opportunities to express my thankfulness in words and in writing.

MANNING THE LIFE BOAT

Don't keep your gratitude to yourself! When you feel thankful for certain people in your life, be bold enough to say it out loud or put it in a letter. One of the great tragedies in life is that too often people just don't know what they mean to each other. You can take one small step toward changing this by writing a letter of gratitude to someone who has touched your life. Name two people you could write a note of thanks to today:

1.

2.

SAIL ON IN PRAYER

God,
When I was a child, my parents
taught me how to say please and thank you,
but now I rarely remember these important words.
Help me to become again like a small child so
I can learn to be thankful all over again.
Thank You, Lord, for my life, for the morning light
and this day. Thank You, Lord,
for giving me what I need so I have something
I can be thankful for.
Amen.

129

GUIDANCE
A LIGHTHOUSE TO GUIDE YOU

Lord, tell me your ways. Show me how to live. Guide me in your truth.
Psalm 25:4–5 NCV

Shannon had never met her guidance counselor. Up until now she'd never had a reason to. But things were getting a little complicated in her life, and she needed an expert opinion. After all, guidance counselors know how to apply to colleges, and Shannon didn't.

After three weeks of waiting for an appointment, Shannon finally found herself face-to-face with her counselor. Pen in hand, she was ready to take notes to get this thing figured out. This was Shannon's chance to get the answers she so desperately needed.

"It's all on the school's Web site," Mr. McMann said. "I'm so sorry no one told you about this."

"Can you show me what to look for on the Web site?" she asked. "I just need you to walk me through it."

Mr. McMann punched a few keys and turned the computer's monitor for Shannon to see. "Everything you need to know is right here. Just follow the path laid out for you."

Sometimes the path is obvious, well-worn, and even straight, right in front of you. Other times it's barely visible or overgrown with weeds, and there might be a fork in the road. For that very reason, God gave us the Bible, a book of instructions as good as any Web site. In it you will find all the instruction you need to live a happy and fulfilling life. And He has also provided a guidance counselor we can rely on—the Holy Spirit—to help us understand all His instructions. He's always waiting to help you any time you call on Him.

CATCHING THE WAVE

Some people think of the Bible as a book of rules. In reality, it is a book of instructions for how to live a successful life. God has included everything you need to live a happy, joyful, useful, fulfilling life. He has also sent the Holy Spirit to help you understand what you are reading and sort out how those instructions apply to you. God has also placed wise people in your path—you probably already know who they are—who can guide you along the way. He wants you to know where to go when you need wisdom and guidance.

SURFING FOR WISDOM

Your ears shall hear a word behind you, saying, "This is the way, walk in it," whenever you turn to the right hand or whenever you turn to the left.
Isaiah 30:21 NKJV

This is what the LORD says—your Redeemer, the Holy One of Israel: "I am the LORD your God, who teaches you what is best for you, who directs you in the way you should go."
Isaiah 48:17

Trust God from the bottom of your heart; don't try to figure out everything on your own. Listen for God's voice in everything you do, everywhere you go; he's the one who will keep you on track.
Proverbs 3:5-6 MSG

I will instruct you and teach you in the way you should go; I will counsel you and watch over you.
Psalm 32:8

DIVING FOR UNDERSTANDING

For hundreds of millions of Americans who believe in God, prayer is our bridge between Earth and Heaven, our way of opening our hearts to the Lord. Through this intimate relationship we find peace and guidance.

Nick Rahall

Before us is a future all unknown, a path untrod; beside us a friend well loved and known—that friend is God.

Anonymous

God speaks to us unceasingly through the events of our lives.

Louis Everly

LIFE SAVER CHALLENGE

I will learn how to follow God's path for my life by:

1. Believing that He has wonderful plans for my life.

2. Reading and studying the Bible to learn the principles of a happy, joyful, fulfilled life.

3. Asking God in prayer for wisdom and instruction as I make important choices.

4. Listening to the advice of godly men and women God has put in my life.

5. Trusting God to show me the best path to take.

MANNING THE LIFE BOAT

You may find yourself to be the one person a friend
confides in when facing a dilemma or challenge. List two sources
of guidance you can share with your friend:

1.

2.

— SAIL ON IN PRAYER —

Lord God,
Thank You for helping me find my way.
The world is so big, and I feel
so small and insignificant at times.
I want my life to count.
I want to be someone who changes things for good.
I want to be a blessing
to the people I love and to You.
Thank You for Your guidance.
Amen.

GUILT
DON'T GO DOWN WITH THE SHIP

Those who are wayward in spirit will gain understanding.
Isaiah 29:24

It was almost midnight on April 14, 1912. Most of the passengers on the luxury liner *Titanic* were already in bed. But the wireless operator was still hard at work sending messages passengers had relayed that day. The operator was so busy that he ignored six incoming messages warning about icebergs in the area. As the saying goes, the rest is history.

Titanic hit an iceberg. An alarm sounded to warn passengers and crew to abandon ship. But many people refused to believe the "unsinkable" *Titanic* could be in trouble and ignored the alarms. The first lifeboat left the ship with 36 empty seats. Some passengers continued to ride stationary bikes in the gym as the ship took on water. Though *Titanic* didn't have enough lifeboats to save everyone, 472 seats remained empty—and 1,503 people died. Imagine how differently this story would have ended if people had paid attention to the warnings they were given.

You have your very own built-in warning system, installed by God. It's called guilt. It's a valuable gift, though it may not feel like it at times. It can make you feel uncomfortable, embarrassed, and full of regret. But that's a good thing. It warns you when you're going the wrong way. If you don't turn around, you could be headed for disaster.

When you feel guilty, don't make a titanic mistake. Heed the warning. Stop what you're doing. Apologize and make things right. Talk to God about what has happened and ask His forgiveness. Then, choose a better direction, so you can keep moving forward, forgiven and guilt-free.

CATCHING THE WAVE

It's easy to confuse guilt
and shame. They can feel
a lot alike. You may feel
an ache in your gut or a
wave of embarrassment.
Then your conscience
sounds the alarm that
something's wrong. With
guilt that alarm says, "I've
made a mistake," or "What
I've done isn't good." With
shame that alarm says,
"I'm a mistake," or "I'm
no good." Guilt is a good
thing. It can motivate you
to make things right. But
shame can lead to depres-
sion. If your shame alarm
won't turn off, tell a youth
pastor or counselor what's
going on. You may need
help accepting God's for-
giveness or dealing with a
deeper issue.

SURFING FOR WISDOM

Create in me a pure heart, O God, and
renew a steadfast spirit within me.
Psalm 51:10

Godly sorrow brings repentance that leads
to salvation and leaves no regret.
2 Corinthians 7:10

There is now no condemnation for those who
are in Christ Jesus, because through Christ
Jesus the law of the Spirit of life set me
free from the law of sin and death.
Romans 8:1-2

Repent, then, and turn to God, so that your
sins may be wiped out, that times of
refreshing may come from the Lord, and
that he may send the Christ, who has been
appointed for you—even Jesus.
Acts 3:19-20

No one whose hope is in you will ever
be put to shame.
Psalm 25:3

LIFE SAVER STORY

Gabriella shared how guilt affected her life:

"When I was six I was exposed to pornography. My sister found my dad's stash and called me in his room to watch it. After having witnessed that, I believe a seed was planted. It took a hold of me, and I really wanted to do the right thing, but I became a slave to it, and I kept giving in to the temptation. I was too scared to turn to someone in fear of what they would say or think of me. I hated myself and felt like God hated me too. I could no longer deal with the guilt and conviction, so I cried out to God asking Him to help me. I didn't know what He could do or how He could do it, but I knew I needed help. God never fails; He gave me strength to resist the temptation."

Is there something in your life that is eating you up with guilt? If so, trust God by telling Him your *story*. If you aren't comfortable writing it here, simply close your eyes and tell Him all about it. Ask for His forgiveness and let Him wash your heart clean.

_____

_____

_____

_____

_____

_____

_____

_____

_____

WHAT IT ALL MEANS

guilt: n., (gĭlt)

Responsibility for a mistake or error; remorseful awareness of having done something wrong; self-reproach for supposed inadequacy or wrongdoing.

4 THINGS TO REMEMBER ABOUT GUILT

1. The guilt that rises up within you is meant to let you know you are doing something wrong.

2. The guilt that is placed on you by the accusatory words of others is most often bogus.

3. When guilt isn't dealt with, it can ruin your relationships with others—even God.

4. The only way to deal with guilt is to take it to God, ask Him to forgive you, and ask Him show you how to make things right.

DIVING FOR UNDERSTANDING

The difference between guilt and shame is very clear—in theory. We feel guilty for what we do. We feel shame for what we are.

Lewis B. Smedes

The purpose of being guilty is to bring us to Jesus. Once we are there, then its purpose is finished.

Corrie ten Boom

You never lose the love of God. Guilt is the warning that temporarily you are out of touch.

Jack Dominion

LIFE SAVER CHALLENGE

If guilt sounds the alarm, I'll take action with these five steps:

1. Make sure I'm dealing with guilt, not shame.

2. Ask God for forgiveness, then forgive myself.

3. Ask forgiveness from anyone I've hurt.

4. Do whatever is in my power to make things right.

5. Ask God to help me not repeat my mistakes.

MANNING THE LIFE BOAT

Do you owe someone an apology? Ask God to give you the right words, and the right time, to express what you need to say. Don't make excuses for what you've done or expect others to apologize in return—even if you feel they should. Just state what you've done, ask for forgiveness, and then move forward from there.

SAIL ON IN PRAYER

Lord God,
Thank You for giving me a conscience
that sounds the alarm when I head
the wrong way. Please help me not to ignore it
but to take action anytime it goes off.
Then, give me the courage to do
what I need to do
to make things right again.
Amen.

HAPPINESS & JOY
ENJOYING THE STORM

Rejoice always.
1 Thessalonians 5:16 NKJV

"Dad?" Phil called out as he poked his head into his father's basement office. "Can I ask you a question?"

"Of course, son," his dad answered.

"Well, I know you've been out of work for, like, six months. Last night I heard you and Mom talking about how you still can't find a job and that we might need to sell our house and move in with Grandpa and Grandma if things don't change. I'm okay with moving, but I just want to know: Why don't you feel stressed? I mean, you seem so happy—and we don't have any money."

Phil's dad leaned forward in his chair and looked him straight in the eyes. "You know, Phil, I used to think owning a home would make me happy. But after we bought this house, I still felt the same. So I bought a new car and a boat. Those things made me happy for a little while, but it didn't last. As soon as the new wore off, the happiness wore off too.

"Now I realize that happiness is just a temporary thing. It comes and goes. Like now, I'm not happy about being out of work. But one day I was reading my Bible and realized that happiness is barely mentioned while the word 'joy' is mentioned a lot—176 times in fact. I found out that happiness is about your circumstances. It's constantly changing. But joy comes from the contentment of knowing that God loves you and accepts you no matter what. My joy sticks around even when we're going through tough times."

CATCHING THE WAVE

Jesus is the source of all joy. That's why your relationship with Him is so important. As you look to Jesus for contentment, you'll discover that the difficult experiences that dragged you down in the past don't affect you as much anymore. In fact, they may not bother you at all. The apostle Paul wrote the book of Philippians from prison—and yet his book is known for being more joyful than any other book in the Bible. Why? Because he knew that God loved him and accepted him. God totally loves and accepts you, and as a result, even when things aren't going your way, you can be joyful.

SURFING FOR WISDOM

[God] will yet fill your mouth with laughter and your lips with shouts of joy.
Job 8:21

I will greatly rejoice in the LORD, my soul shall be joyful in my God.
Isaiah 61:10 NKJV

Let all who take refuge in you be glad; let them ever sing for joy. Spread your protection over them, that those who love your name may rejoice in you.
Psalm 5:11

May the God of hope fill you with all joy and peace as you trust in him, so that you may overflow with hope by the power of the Holy Spirit.
Romans 15:13

The joy of the LORD will make you strong.
Nehemiah 8:10 NCV

LIFE SAVER

DIVING FOR UNDERSTANDING

Life need not be easy to be joyful. Joy is not the absence of trouble but the presence of Christ.

William Van der Hoten

Happiness is caused by things that happen around me, and circumstances will mar it; but joy flows right on through trouble. Joy flows on through the day; joy flows in the night as well as in the day; joy flows through persecution and opposition. It is an unceasing fountain bubbling up in the heart; a secret spring the world can't see and doesn't know anything about.

Dwight L. Moody

Joy is the most infallible sign of the presence of God.

Leon Bloy

LIFE SAVER CHALLENGE

I will let my life explode with joy by pursuing the following steps:

1. Whenever I get discouraged, I will remind myself that true joy and contentment only come from knowing Jesus.

2. Write Philippians 4:4 on an index card and tape it to my bathroom mirror or the inside of my bedroom door.

3. Read the book of Philippians, remembering that Paul wrote it from a prison cell.

MANNING THE LIFE BOAT

No matter what purpose God has for your life, it will include reaching out in some way to help others. Name two ways you can share with others the joy that only comes from God:

1.

2.

SAIL ON IN PRAYER

Dear Jesus,
It's so easy to believe
that convincing people to accept me
or getting more stuff will make me happy.
Lord, now I know it will never be enough.
Please give me the joy of knowing
that You completely love and accept me.
Amen.

HONESTY
SAILING ON COURSE

Do not lie. Do not deceive one another.
Leviticus 19:11

The president of the business club was considered a plum enhancement for students seeking to improve their chances of getting into a top school after graduation. Each year, a junior was chosen to serve as president during his or her senior year. Because the competition was so fierce, a team of instructors was given the task of carefully considering each candidate's merits and selecting three who would then be voted on by the other members of the club. Gregg had planned his strategy well, joining the club as a freshman and taking an unofficial leadership role early on. He was sure he was a shoe-in.

During the selection process, the students had lunch with the instructors, an informal, get-acquainted time. One of the instructors happened to be behind Gregg in the cafeteria line and watched as he hid a small 25-cent square of butter under his napkin where the cashier wouldn't see it.

That afternoon, the selection team summoned Gregg to the business school conference room. He entered with a hopeful smile on his face, letting his mind wander to his future at the college of his choice. The smile vanished when the team told him he was no longer being considered.

"Honesty isn't a selective quality," the team leader announced. "People who lie about little things tend to lie about big things as well. If you would sacrifice honesty for a 25-cent pad of butter, you'd sacrifice it for other things."

Whatever you find yourself doing in life, do it with absolute honesty. Be truthful even about the small details. Be *consistently* honest. You and those you interact with will appreciate the dividends that the truth brings.

CATCHING THE WAVE

Steve wasn't the most talented or the most popular person at the small company where he worked after school. But whenever the boss faced a dilemma or was anxious about what was going on with his employees, he called on Steve. The reason? For all his flaws, Steve always told the truth. He never told the boss what he thought he wanted to hear. He didn't color the truth to his own advantage, and he wasn't swayed by the opinions of others.

If you can be trusted to tell the truth, you will be the kind of friend, coworker, and significant other that everyone needs and wants. In fact, people will be willing to overlook a lot of other faults in exchange for one of the world's rarest traits: unflinching honesty.

SURFING FOR WISDOM

The LORD hates anyone who cheats, but he likes everyone who is honest.
Proverbs 11:1 CEV

Good people will be guided by honesty.
Proverbs 11:3 NCV

"These are the things you are to do: Speak the truth to each other, and render true and sound judgment in your courts; do not plot evil against your neighbor, and do not love to swear falsely. I hate all this," declares the LORD.
Zechariah 8:16-17

A light shines in the dark for honest people, for those who are merciful and kind and good.
Psalm 112:4 NCV

LIFE SAVER

DIVING FOR UNDERSTANDING

A true friend will tell you the truth to your face—not behind your back.
Sasha Azevedo

Honesty is the cornerstone of all success, without which confidence and ability to perform shall cease to exist.
Mary Kay Ash

We tell lies when we are afraid ... afraid of what we don't know, afraid of what others will think, afraid of what will be found out about us. But every time we tell a lie, the thing that we fear grows stronger.
Tad Williams

LIFE SAVER CHALLENGE

I will strive to make honesty one of the hallmarks of my life by:

1. Praying that God will give me the courage and clarity of mind to consistently tell the truth.

2. Thinking before I speak, especially when I'm on the "hot seat."

3. Remembering that dishonesty is a progressive disease. One lie always leads to more.

4. Keeping in mind that honesty will help people trust me and value me.

5. Reminding myself—every time I'm tempted to lie—that each lie I tell will erode someone's trust in me.

MANNING THE LIFE BOAT

While lies and liars often grab the headlines, an honest person grabs something much more important: trust. If you can be a bright ray of honesty among the dark clouds of lies, people around you will wonder what is behind your commitment to being truthful. This could give you an opportunity to share your faith. And when you do, your listeners will believe what you're telling them because of the trust you've earned.

SAIL ON IN PRAYER

Dear God,
It's scary how easily a lie
comes out of my mouth.
Sometimes it seems like I have to pay
extra attention just to be sure
I'm telling the truth.
I know that Jesus told the truth
all the time,
no matter what.
Help me to be more like Him.
Amen.

HOPE
AN ANCHOR THAT HOLDS

God rewrote the text of my life when I opened the book of my heart to his eyes.
Psalm 18:24 MSG

Josh was only five days old when his mother died. His father remarried a few years later. But Josh's new stepmother was an alcoholic who beat him repeatedly when his father was away. When Josh's father found out what was going on, he divorced Josh's stepmother. But the damage had already been done. By sixth grade, Josh was taking drugs and getting into fights. Then, a drunk driver caused the death of his best friend. The next year, another friend died in the same way. Overwhelmed by grief and anger, Josh tried to take his own life. He didn't succeed. But by this time, Josh could only focus on what had been lost. Hope was one of the things on that long list.

After being arrested, Josh wound up at House of Hope in Orlando, Florida. There, Josh discovered he wasn't hopeless. He was treasured. He was loved. When Josh came to believe in God, he realized God also believed in him. God knew Josh's story, but that story was still being written. With God's help, Josh wrote a new chapter by changing the direction of his life.

Circumstances can be unpredictable. People aren't always loving. Your own strength and abilities can let you down. But you can always count on God. He keeps every promise He's ever made. No matter what's happened in the past, you can hold on to the hope of a brand-new tomorrow. So much more of your story has yet to be written. Place your hope in God. He's an anchor that holds firm, no matter how wild the waves.

CATCHING THE WAVE

Suppose you were marooned on a desert island. You might eventually lose hope of being rescued. But what if someone who cared about you knew your location and promised to send help? In that case, you could stop worrying about tomorrow. You could rest in the fact that help was on its way, even if you couldn't see that ship on the horizon. Placing your hope in God works the same way. You can hope in His promises to heal, help, love, and forgive. Even if you can't see the solution yet, you can rest in the fact that God is at work.

SURFING FOR WISDOM

No one whose hope is in you will ever be put to shame.
Psalm 25:3

He shall strengthen your heart, all you who hope in the LORD.
Psalm 31:24 NKJV

Our soul waits for the LORD; he is our help and shield. Our heart is glad in him, because we trust in his holy name. Let your steadfast love, O LORD, be upon us, even as we hope in you.
Psalm 33:20-22 NRSV

May the God of hope fill you with all joy and peace in believing, so that you may abound in hope by the power of the Holy Spirit.
Romans 15:13 NRSV

LIFE SAVER STORY

Danae shared this story:

"I grew up with my dad abusing me. Things at my school were not going well, and I was being bullied for not being the coolest. I felt so hopeless I started cutting and wanted to commit suicide. Soon after I started struggling with an eating disorder. My parents divorced, and my life continued on a downward spiral. Everyone thought I was good, but the truth was I was falling apart. One day my mom took me to church, and the pastor was talking about how Jesus could give hope. I knew this Jesus guy was who I needed. I accepted Him into my heart and started making friends who built me up. Things haven't been perfect since accepting Jesus, but I do have hope. I encourage anyone that feels hopeless to reach out to someone for help and get plugged in to a church that will build you up."

Do you feel hopeless? Do you feel sometimes like you are doomed and nothing will ever change? Do you need the hope Jesus can give? What is your story?

_____

_____

_____

_____

_____

_____

_____

_____

WHAT IT ALL MEANS

hope: n., (hōp)

The feeling that what is wanted can be had or that events will turn out for the best; a person or thing in which expectations are centered; something that is hoped for.

hope: v.

To look forward to with desire and reasonable confidence; to believe, desire, or trust; to feel that something desired may happen; to place trust; rely.

4 WAYS GOD GIVES US HOPE

1. By removing the burden of our guilt and shame.

2. By promising us the comfort of His constant presence in our lives.

3. By assuring us that we can achieve great things with His help.

4. By presenting us with the gift of eternal life.

LIFE SAVER

DIVING FOR UNDERSTANDING

Hope is an adventure, a going forward—a confident search for a rewarding life.
Karl Menninger

Behind the cloud the starlight lurks, through showers the sunbeams fall; for God, who loveth all his works, has left his hope with all!
John Greenleaf Whittier

Most of the important things in the world have been accomplished by people who have kept on trying when there seemed to be no hope at all.
Dale Carnegie

LIFE SAVER CHALLENGE

There will be days when you feel hopeless and helpless. Prepare for them before they happen by keeping a list of promises from the Bible in a notebook or journal. **When you read or hear a Bible promise you want to remember, add it to your list.** Begin by writing down *Psalm 145:13, 2 Peter 3:8–9, Isaiah 65:24, Psalm 33:18, and John 3:16.*

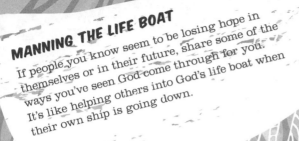

MANNING THE LIFE BOAT

If people you know seem to be losing hope in themselves or in their future, share some of the ways you've seen God come through for you. It's like helping others into God's life boat when their own ship is going down.

— SAIL ON IN PRAYER —

Lord God,
I want to look forward to what's ahead
without being afraid or discouraged.
But I get so distracted by how I feel
and anything that seems to go wrong.
Help me place my hope in You.
You're the only one I can count on
to never fail.
Amen.

LONELINESS
A BRIDGE OVER TROUBLED WATERS

**I am always with you;
you hold me by my right hand.**
Psalm 73:23

Sandra loved going to her neighborhood coffee shop before school. It was the one place where everyone knew her name. The baristas started making her quad skinny caramel espresso before she even crossed the threshold. They smiled and asked her whether her chemistry teacher was still a pain. They kept track of how many days until summer. Sandra wished she could feel as visible in her school as she did in this coffee shop.

As high schools go, Lakeview High was large, boasting more than 2,000 students. The school tried to make it easier for students to adjust to a large school by offering dozens of clubs, but for many it still felt like an impersonal sea of bodies moving from class to class. Sandra walked those halls believing she was a ghost—unseen and unknown. She would often catch a glimpse of other "spirits" across the courtyard or in a corner of the library. They felt the same way she did, but no one wanted to acknowledge it. They felt alone in the midst of thousands.

There's a difference between being alone and being lonely. You can be at your best friend's party and still feel completely alone. You may think no one notices you. The truth is that the God of the universe, the Maker of heaven and earth, notices. In fact, He knows you by name. He is always there, sight unseen, in your midst. He's waiting for you to notice Him from across the crowded room. Who do you think led Sandra to that coffee shop?

CATCHING THE WAVE

Even in the midst of trouble that no one else can understand, you are not alone. Sometimes feeling alone or finding yourself alone is exactly where God wants you to be. Sometimes, only then will you take notice of the one who's been right there, in front of you all the time. He'll do whatever it takes to get your attention. Yes, sometimes He allows you to feel alone in a crowd so you might reach out for Him. When finally you take His hand, He'll lead you to those who notice, those who can chase away your loneliness.

SURFING FOR WISDOM

Sing to God, sing praise to his name, extol him who rides on the clouds—his name is the LORD—and rejoice before him. A father to the fatherless, a defender of widows, is God in his holy dwelling. God sets the lonely in families, he leads forth the prisoners with singing.
Psalm 68:4-6

God has said, "Never will I leave you; never will I forsake you."
Hebrews 13:5

I am convinced that neither death nor life, neither angels nor demons, neither the present nor the future, nor any powers, neither height nor depth, nor anything else in all creation, will be able to separate us from the love of God that is in Christ Jesus our Lord.
Romans 8:38-39

The LORD your God goes with you; he will never leave you nor forsake you.
Deuteronomy 31:6

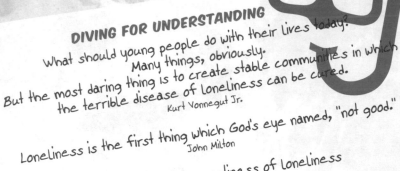

DIVING FOR UNDERSTANDING

What should young people do with their lives today?
Many things, obviously.
But the most daring thing is to create stable communities in which
the terrible disease of loneliness can be cured.
Kurt Vonnegut Jr.

Loneliness is the first thing which God's eye named, "not good."
John Milton

To transform the emptiness of loneliness
to the fullness of aloneness.
Ah, that is the secret of life.
Sunita Khosia

LIFE SAVER CHALLENGE

I will break the bonds of loneliness by:

1. Talking to God every day about my life and including Him in it.

2. Being the one to invite someone else to join me instead of
waiting to be invited.

3. Enjoying time alone and seeing it as a chance to focus on what's
important to me.

4. Realizing that when it is quiet, I can hear God.

MANNING THE LIFE BOAT

Loneliness is not always visible. You can't always recognize it by looking at someone. Ask God to show you two people you can include in something you're doing today.

1.

2.

SAIL ON IN PRAYER

Lord God,
I am alone in the midst of so many people.
No one knows my pain. No one would understand.
Please don't be silent.
Turn Your ear to my cry and lift me out
of my loneliness. Show Yourself to me
and show me how to reach out to those
around me who are also lonely.
Amen.

LOVE & ROMANCE

ABOUT THAT LIFEGUARD YOU'VE BEEN WATCHING ...

Greet one another with a kiss of love.

1 Peter 5:14 NRSV

"Love makes the world go 'round." At least that's what they say. Turn on the television, and you're likely to find a show about love. The same goes with the music on your iPod or the movies you watch with your friends.

Movies, songs, books, and music videos often represent love as something that will make us happy forever, satisfy every longing, and fill every hole in our hearts. "Just find the right person," they tell us, "and all of your problems will go away." When some people realize that the person they're in a relationship with can't fill the hole in their heart or that they still have problems, they move on to the next person in search of the perfect relationship. But that kind of love simply doesn't exist, at least not between two people.

Only God's love will satisfy you completely. Yet God has designed you to enjoy a romantic love that you will one day share with that special someone. The kind of love that lasts doesn't begin with expecting something from the other person; it begins with giving. Rather than look to the other person to make them happy, those who experience true love seek to serve that person. Real love respects, trusts, and never seeks to take advantage of the other person. Most importantly, it remains committed, even after the heart-thumping feelings go away.

This is a love worth waiting for. Be sure you seek the real thing rather than settling for a mirage—the kind of love that doesn't really exist.

CATCHING THE WAVE

While being in a relationship can be exciting, the Bible encourages us to be careful not to awaken love until the right time. That means you should take it slow in your relationships. You don't need a serious boyfriend or girlfriend just yet. And getting sexually involved with another person at this point is asking for trouble. Wait until your heart can handle it. As you get older, your heart will be able to deal with the intensity of serious relationships. Finally, when you get married, you'll be able to enjoy all the benefits of love and sexual attraction.

SURFING FOR WISDOM

Love is patient and kind. Love is not jealous, it does not brag, and it is not proud. Love is not rude, is not selfish, and does not get upset with others. Love does not count up wrongs that have been done.
1 Corinthians 13:4-5 NCV

Hatred stirs up dissension, but love covers over all wrongs.
Proverbs 10:12

Happy are those who live pure lives, who follow the LORD's teachings.
Psalm 119:1 NCV

[Jesus said,] "They are blessed whose thoughts are pure, for they will see God."
Matthew 5:8 NCV

DIVING FOR UNDERSTANDING

You come to love not by finding the perfect person,
but by seeing an imperfect person perfectly.
Sam Keen

Love is the condition in which the happiness of another person
is essential to your own.
Robert A. Heinlein

No one who hurts you is worth your tears,
and when you find someone who is worth your tears,
that person won't make you cry.
Anonymous

LIFE SAVER CHALLENGE

I will prepare my heart for true love by:

1. **Enjoying friendships with lots of people of the opposite sex rather than just one person.**

2. **Avoiding heart-damaging situations that may tempt me to get sexually involved with someone.**

3. **Learning about true love from married couples who love God.**

4. **Praying that God will prepare my heart for the person I may someday marry—and asking God to prepare the other person's heart for me!**

MANNING THE LIFE BOAT

As you grow in your understanding of love and relationships, make sure to share what you've learned with your friends. Name two ways you can pass it along.

1.

2.

— **SAIL ON IN PRAYER** —

Dear God,
I need Your help to grow
a healthy heart that understands
the meaning of true love.
Please give me the wisdom
and strength I need to protect it
from being damaged by giving in to
sexual temptation. Thank You for loving me
with a love that will never
let me go.
Amen.

MERCY & KINDNESS

WHEN MERCY FALLS LIKE RAIN

It is good to be merciful and generous.

Psalm 112:5 NCV

On a lonely Illinois road, 16-year-old Thomas Weller struggled to make his way home in a blizzard. But the slick roads and blowing snow won out. He plowed into a snow bank, leaving him helplessly stuck on a freezing night.

Shaken but unhurt, Thomas sat in his car and waited. Unfortunately, he seemed to be the only person around.

Finally, someone stopped—a man who happened to have a tow chain. He freed Thomas's car, and the grateful teenager made it home. Later that night, Thomas realized: *There wasn't any other traffic tonight. That man probably saved my life.*

Whether or not that act of mercy saved Thomas's life, it certainly changed it. Today, at age 61, Thomas, known as the "San Diego Highwayman," pilots his custom-built '55 Ford Country Wagon/'56 Crown Vic hybrid in the vicinity of his San Diego home, scanning roadsides for stranded motorists. He's been on this mission of mercy for 45 years, ever since his encounter with the Illinois snow bank. An auto mechanic by trade, Thomas has made more than 6,000 roadside assists, filling up empty gas tanks, changing flat tires, and pouring coolant into hissing radiators.

He accepts no pay for his services. He asks only that those he helps pass it along by lending a hand the next time they encounter someone in distress.

Long ago, Jesus delivered a stirring sermon to a crowd on a mountainside. He proclaimed, "Blessed are the merciful, for they will be shown mercy." Thomas Weller's life exemplifies this truth. Does yours?

CATCHING THE WAVE

One of the most amazing things about mercy is that it's a gift that keeps on giving. Imagine how different our world would be if each person who received an act of mercy passed it along to someone else. Millions of lives would be changed for the better. And mercy is something every person, no matter how young or old, has the ability to give. That may not involve helping stranded motorists, but if you're paying attention, you will find many opportunities to help others and make the world a better place.

SURFING FOR WISDOM

[Jesus began to teach them, saying,]
"Blessed are the merciful,
for they will be shown mercy."
Matthew 5:7

[Jesus said to his disciples,] "Be merciful,
just as your Father is merciful."
Luke 6:36

[God] saved us, not because of righteous
things we had done, but because of
his mercy. He saved us through the washing
of rebirth and renewal by the Holy Spirit.
Titus 3:5

Mercy, peace and love be yours
in abundance.
Jude 2

LIFE SAVER STORY

Ridley wanted us to hear this story:

"If you are trying to reach out to the ones in your community that are going through depression, I know how you feel. It's not easy. I used to be the one that everyone talked to and really had no problem in my social life. But one day I found one of my close friends bullying a small quiet kid. I did not know how to react. So at lunch I had one of my true faithful brothers in Christ come with me to sit by this kid.

"Everyone thought we were crazy, but we sat by that kid and talked to him every day after that. Each day he talked more and more. One day at lunch he told me we had stopped him from committing suicide. He said we were the only people he could open up to and trust. Now he goes to Bible study with me, and his life has been changed. That just shows how a little kindness can change someone's life."

Has giving or receiving mercy made a difference in your life? What is your story?

_____

_____

_____

_____

_____

_____

_____

WHAT IT ALL MEANS

mer cy: n. (mur see)

Compassionate or kindly forbearance shown toward an offender, an enemy, or other person in one's power; compassion, pity, or benevolence; the disposition to be compassionate or forbearing; an act of kindness, compassion, or favor; something that gives evidence of divine favor; blessing.

3 MIRACLES THAT FOLLOW ACTS OF MERCY

1. The course of a person's life can be changed from doom and darkness to hope and light.

2. The cycle of anger and revenge can be broken.

3. Love can destroy hatred and mend broken relationships.

LIFE SAVER

DIVING FOR UNDERSTANDING

The quality of mercy is not strained; it droppeth as the gentle rain from heaven upon the place beneath. It is twice blessed—it blesseth him that gives, and him that takes.

William Shakespeare

All the great things are simple, and many can be expressed in a single word: freedom, justice, honor, duty, mercy, hope.

Winston Churchill

Teach me to feel another's woe, to hide the fault I see, that mercy I to others show, that mercy show to me.

Alexander Pope

LIFE SAVER CHALLENGE

I will be a more merciful person by:

1. Committing to be the one who helps a person in need—not assuming that "someone else will do it."

2. Not demanding revenge when I'm wronged but showing mercy instead.

3. Paying it forward every time I am the beneficiary of an act of kindness or mercy.

4. Treating others as I would like to be treated, especially in times of hardship or grief.

MANNING THE LIFE BOAT

Have you heard the adage, "People don't care how much you know until they know how much you care"? As clever remarks go, that's a pretty good one. It expresses the underlying reason why Christian relief agencies often provide food, medical services, and education to communities they work with in developing nations. These agencies also share the good news of Jesus with people, but they know it's hard to focus on a sermon when you're starving or sick.

In the same way, if you want people to pay attention to you when you share your faith, you have to earn that attention through your kindness, mercy, and caring heart. People respond to a brand of faith that they see put into action in everyday life.

SAIL ON IN PRAYER

Dear God,
I know how good it feels
when someone shows me kindness,
especially when that kindness is undeserved or
unexpected. Help me to avoid hoarding those good,
warm feelings. Inspire me to show mercy every time I
get the chance. Help me to remember that one
good deed from me can make someone's
whole day—and maybe
even change a life.
Amen.

MONEY
THE HIGH SEAS

Rich and poor have this in common: The LORD is the Maker of them all.

Proverbs 22:2

Matt turned on his mother's computer and waited what seemed like a century for it to boot up. Dialing up on the Internet took even longer. It seemed like as soon as he got ready to work, the computer would lock up and he'd have to go through the process all over again.

"Mom, how do you expect me to do my school work on that stupid dinosaur of a computer? It's bad enough that we still have dial-up for the Internet, but that old junker is a joke!" Matt whined.

"Sorry, Matt. I told you we'd get you a laptop for graduation so you'll have something better to take to college," his mother said.

"But Mom, what's the difference? I graduate in four weeks anyway."

"Laptops are expensive, Matt, and we just don't have the money right now. I thought you understood that," his mother reminded him.

Matt kept trying until he was able to get online. That's when he saw the e-mail from his friend Jason asking him to run a 5K race with him in honor of his mother.

Jason had his own laptop and his own car. But Jason no longer had a mother. She had died of breast cancer. *I bet Jason would trade everything he has to have his mom back*, Matt thought.

"Whoa, and I love you too," Matt's mom said with a giggle as he came up behind her and gave her a big hug.

CATCHING THE WAVE

Too often we long for the things we don't have and take for granted the priceless gifts God has placed in our lives. It's a good thing to be reminded that money is limited in what it can do. The truly important, lasting things like family, true friendship, and respect can't be purchased at any price, though many have tried to buy them. Your attitude about money will affect every area of your life.

SURFING FOR WISDOM

Keep your lives free from the love of money and be content with what you have.
Hebrews 13:5

[Jesus] went on, "Take care! Protect yourself against the least bit of greed. Life is not defined by what you have, even when you have a lot."
Luke 12:15 MSG

Warn the rich people of this world not to be proud or to trust in wealth that is easily lost.
1 Timothy 6:17 CEV

LIFE SAVER

DIVING FOR UNDERSTANDING

Money never made a man happy yet,
nor will it. The more a man has,
the more he wants. Instead of filling a vacuum,
it makes one.

Benjamin Franklin

If a person gets his attitude toward money straight, it will help
straighten out almost every other area of his life.

Billy Graham

With money you can buy a house, but not a home; a clock,
but not time; a bed but not sleep; a book, but not knowledge;
a doctor, but not health; a position, but not respect; blood, but not
life; sex, but not love.

Chinese Proverb

LIFE SAVER CHALLENGE

I will learn to focus less on money and what it can buy by:

1. Asking God to reveal to me if I've made money too important in my life.

2. Looking around me to see who has a need that my money or my stuff can help.

3. Giving some of what I make to a charity or church of my choice.

4. Being grateful for what God has provided and thanking Him daily.

MANNING THE LIFE BOAT

Giving is the best way to keep your attitude about money balanced. Prevent a selfish attitude by giving of your time, talent, and treasure. Name one way for each that you can do tomorrow:

1.

2.

3.

SAIL ON IN PRAYER

Heavenly Father,
Thank You for helping me keep money
in its place in my life,
not allowing it to tell me what is
or is not important.
I know You are watching over me
and You will provide what I need.
Amen.

PAIN & HEALING
THE HEALING TIDES

The LORD is close to the brokenhearted; he rescues those whose spirits are crushed.
Psalm 34:18 NLT

Pain is an attention-seeker. It demands the spotlight. Whether your pain is physical or emotional, it can get in the way of your plans. At times, it can even change your life—for the better. It did for Greg Woodburn. Sidelined from high school track by knee and hip injuries, Greg was feeling pretty low. All he wanted to do was run. Then Greg's sister reminded him that some people weren't running because they didn't even have shoes. That got Greg thinking, and then it got him up and moving.

Though it took time for Greg's physical injuries to heal, he used that time well. He collected running shoes, cleaned them up, and donated them to those in need, starting with an orphanage in Uganda. Four years later, Greg is running again. Yes, sometimes it's on the track. But he's also running a nonprofit organization. To date, Greg's organization, Give Running, has donated more than 6,000 pairs of gently used shoes to needy children around the world.

Pain can draw all of your attention inward. It can make you focus on yourself. At first, that's a good thing. Pain pressures you into doing what you can to relieve it, to help heal it. But once you've done what you can, whether you're fully healed or not, it's time to refocus. It's time to see what lessons pain has for you to learn. It's easy to get caught up in what hurts, instead of using your pain to discover what helps. With God's help, everything—even pain—can be the start of something good.

CATCHING THE WAVE

During the last three years of Jesus' life, the two things He seemed to spend most of His time doing were telling people about His Father in heaven and healing those who were hurting. Pain matters to God. He cares when His children suffer. He cares so much that He doesn't want those hard times to go to waste. He wants to use them to help open His children's eyes and hearts to things they might not notice when life is going well. When you're hurting, remember God is near. Call on Him for comfort and healing. Then ask Him, "What do you want me to learn while I'm here?"

SURFING FOR WISDOM

Friends, when life gets really difficult, don't jump to the conclusion that God isn't on the job. Instead, be glad that you are in the very thick of what Christ experienced. This is a spiritual refining process, with glory just around the corner.
1 Peter 4:12-13 MSG

"I will restore you to health and heal your wounds," declares the LORD.
Jeremiah 30:17

This is what the LORD says, ... "I will heal my people and will let them enjoy abundant peace and security."
Jeremiah 33:7,6

Unto you that fear my name shall the Sun of righteousness arise with healing in his wings ... saith the LORD.
Malachi 4:2-3 KJV

I am the LORD who heals you.
Exodus 15:26 NRSV

173

LIFE SAVER

DIVING FOR UNDERSTANDING

Pain is something to carry, like a radio. You feel your strength in the experience of pain. It's all in how you carry it. That's what matters.
Jim Morrison

Wisdom is nothing more than healed pain.
Robert Gary Lee

Painful as it may be, a significant emotional event can be the catalyst for choosing a direction that serves us—and those around us—more effectively. Look for the learning.
Louisa May Alcott

LIFE SAVER CHALLENGE

When I'm in pain, I'll begin the healing process with these five steps:

1. Pay attention to my pain. (Ignoring it won't make it go away!)

2. Ask God to heal my pain.

3. Seek help from a counselor or medical professional if my pain won't heal.

4. Ask God to reveal any lessons my pain has to teach me.

5. Act on any lesson I learn.

MANNING THE LIFE BOAT

When you're hurting, helping others is like a two-for-one special. It helps take your mind off your own pain. Brainstorm one specific way to help someone in need. Write it below. Then put love and pain relief into action by carrying it out.

_____

_____

_____

_____

SAIL ON IN PRAYER

Lord God,
I'm hurting.
I know that You love me so much
that whatever hurts me also hurts You.
Please remove this pain from my life.
I need Your comfort and Your healing.
Show me how to see beyond my own hurt to what
You want me to learn during this time.
Amen.

PATIENCE
WATER IN YOUR FACE

Patience is better than strength.

Proverbs 16:32 NCV

"I just want to scream!" Jessica sobbed to Alicia over the phone. "My parents made me babysit Caleb this afternoon when this was the only day this week that I could hang out with you at the mall. Then, while I was watching him, he snuck into my bedroom and smeared my mascara all over the carpet. My mom told me to keep all my makeup in the bathroom, so I'm in big trouble. I just want to hurt him!"

"Now take a deep breath and calm down," Alicia began. "It's not the end of the world. You just need to be a little more patient." By the time Alicia finished talking, Jessica felt much better.

Little brothers can test anyone's patience. So can waiting to get un-grounded or killing time before getting your driver's license. Instead of acting on your feelings and doing something you'll later regret, be like Jessica. Apart from leaving her makeup in her bedroom, she *did* make a wise choice: Instead of going off on her brother, she talked to a friend. Alicia also offered some sound advice: She counseled her friend to take a deep breath before doing something that would make matters worse.

If you're a follower of Jesus, then Jesus lives in you. That means He's such a big part of your life that He can give you the patience you need to handle any situation. You just might need someone to remind you about that every now and then.

CATCHING THE WAVE

Patience is different from not getting angry or not getting even. It means controlling your emotions so you can respond the way God wants you to respond. The Bible says the patience that comes from God is a fruit of the Spirit. In other words, it's a result of the Holy Spirit working in your life. When you feel as if you've run out of patience, ask God to share some of His patience with you—and then remember the different ways He shows you patience every day.

SURFING FOR WISDOM

God will strengthen you with his own great power. And you will not give up when troubles come, but you will be patient.
Colossians 1:11 ICB

Be completely humble and gentle; be patient, bearing with one another in love.
Ephesians 4:2

Be patient when trouble comes, and pray at all times.
Romans 12:12 NCV

Since God chose you to be the holy people he loves, you must clothe yourselves with tenderhearted mercy, kindness, humility, gentleness, and patience.
Colossians 3:12 NLT

We also pray that you will be strengthened with all his glorious power so you will have all the endurance and patience you need.
Colossians 1:11 NLT

DIVING FOR UNDERSTANDING

Patience is the ability to idle your motor when you feel like stripping your gears.
Barbara Johnson

Patience serves as a protection against wrongs as clothes do against cold. For if you put on more clothes as the cold increases, it will have no power to hurt you. So in like manner you must grow in patience when you meet with great wrongs, and they will then be powerless to vex your mind.
Leonardo da Vinci

I have just three things to teach: simplicity, patience, compassion. These three are your greatest treasures.
Lao Tzu

LIFE SAVER CHALLENGE

I will strengthen my patience "muscles" by following these four steps:

1. Taking a deep breath and counting to 10 before saying or doing anything I may regret later.

2. Asking God for patience when I feel I'm about to lose control of my emotions.

3. Talking to a levelheaded friend about what I'm feeling inside.

4. Remembering the many ways God shows His patience with me.

MANNING THE LIFE BOAT

You likely have friends who need a little patience too. Name two ways you can help other people strengthen their patience "muscles."

1.

2.

— SAIL ON IN PRAYER —

Dear Jesus,
Sometimes I feel so overwhelmed
by my emotions.
Please give me the patience
to treat people the way You treat me.
Thank You for coming to live in me
and giving me the strength I need
to be like You.
Amen.

PEACE & CONFLICT
PEACE IN THE STORM

Christ himself is our peace.
Ephesians 2:14 NCV

Katie Brown weighs only 95 pounds and measures just a bit over five feet. She stands a lot taller than that, however, once she's nimbly scaled a 100-foot climbing wall—the equivalent of a 10-story building.

Katie's event is "difficulty climbing," an endeavor in which she's a world champion and multiple gold medalist at the "X Games," which you may have seen televised on networks like ESPN2.

As you might imagine, it's intimidating for a small person to attack climbing walls and cliffs that are 20 times her height, but Katie says that her relationship with God brings her peace, even amid extremely dangerous challenges. "I know that I couldn't have done what I've done without being a Christian," she explains. "My faith in God doesn't get rid of my healthy fear of climbing extreme heights, but it does help me deal with it. It takes away a lot of the pressure, because you know that God's not going to condemn you if you don't win. So there's nothing to worry about."

The "walls" you face in your life might not be physical walls. They may be emotional or relational walls. And it's OK to feel intimidated or frightened by the walls in your life. As Katie noted, it would be unhealthy *not* to appreciate the significance of a major challenge.

But, like Katie, you can find peace and security in the truth that God is with you always, and He won't condemn you if you can't get to the top of your wall—even if it takes you hundreds of attempts. God is more concerned with your faithful effort and being your companion as you scale the challenges in your life.

CATCHING THE WAVE

Years ago, a woman created a painting that portrayed her husband leaning into a heavy wind and driving rain during a spring thunderstorm. In one arm, the man cuddled his infant daughter, using his overcoat to shield her from the elements. Despite the storm, the baby was sleeping soundly. The woman titled her painting PEACE.

In life, true peace, peace of the heart, isn't about the absence of problems. It's all about the presence of a loving heavenly Father who is with us always. And He is especially close to us when life's storms rage all around us.

SURFING FOR WISDOM

You, LORD, give true peace to those who depend on you, because they trust you.
Isaiah 26:3 NCV

The fruit of righteousness will be peace; the effect of righteousness will be quietness and confidence forever.
Isaiah 32:17

I will both lie down and sleep in peace; for you alone, O LORD, make me lie down in safety.
Psalm 4:8 NRSV

Do not be anxious about anything, but in everything, by prayer and petition, with thanksgiving, present your requests to God. And the peace of God, which transcends all understanding, will guard your hearts and your minds in Christ Jesus.
Philippians 4:6-7

God is not the author of confusion, but of peace.
1 Corinthians 14:33 KJV

DIVING FOR UNDERSTANDING

To be at one with God is to be at peace ... peace is to be found only within, and unless one finds it there he will never find it at all. Peace lies not in the external world. It lies within one's own soul.
Ralph Waldo Trine

First keep the peace within yourself, then you can also bring peace to others.
Thomas à Kempis

There may be those on earth who dress better or eat better, but those who enjoy the peace of God sleep better.
L. Thomas Holdcroft

LIFE SAVER CHALLENGE

I will pursue peace of mind and heart by:

1. Focusing on my all-powerful God in times of trouble, rather than being overwhelmed by circumstances.

2. Praying that peace will rule my heart.

3. Seeking out someone who always seems at peace regardless of circumstances and asking, "How do you do that?"

4. Finding a favorite scripture about peace—one that I can rely on and use in prayer and meditation in difficult times.

5. Finding songs that calm my heart—and listening to them or singing them to quiet my spirit.

MANNING THE LIFE BOAT

If the peace of Jesus is the calming, stabilizing influence in your life, it will open doors for you to reach out to others. In a world with so much noise and discord, peace is a treasure you can help someone discover.

SAIL ON IN PRAYER

Dear God,
I know You are the source of true peace,
and You can give me peace no matter what's
going on around me. That's what I want, Lord.
Help me to remember that You are
with me wherever I go,
and Your peace is always with me too,
if I just stop and wait for it.
Amen.

PEER PRESSURE

UNDERTOW

Be strong in the Lord and in his mighty power.
Ephesians 6:10

Donna couldn't wait to get out of the house and crash at her cousin's for break. Her parents were just too much in her business right now, and she wanted an escape.

When we got to her cousin Kelly's house, Kelly bounded into the room like a Great Dane ready to play. "Come with me," she beckoned.

"Hello to you, too," Donna said and followed her up the stairs to the third-floor attic. They were greeted by a dozen of Kelly's closest friends. They sat together in a circle with a pile of chips and cans of soda in a bucket of ice in the middle. The music put her right as rain.

By the time Donna saw them passing the joint it, was too late. This wasn't the escape she was looking for. Her mind raced for something to say that wouldn't be lame, yet would get her out of there.

"I don't want to do this," she whispered to her favorite cousin. "I want to go home."

"Don't embarrass me," Kelly scolded.

Don't embarrass you? Donna thought. "I'm out of here."

Her mom showed up within 10 minutes of her call. "Do you want to talk about it?" she asked.

"Not now," Donna said, but she was glad her mom asked.

God will always offer you a way of escape. It just may not always look like what you'd expect. When you find yourself in over your head, reach up, and God will pull you out. It's not lame to walk away; it's brave.

CATCHING THE WAVE

The Bible says that you can know the character of a person by who they hang out with. You start by talking to them, then standing with them, and then finally sitting with them. Try not to get washed away by a situation that is too strong for you to fight. If you sense that the situation is leading you in the wrong direction, take that opportunity to ask for help and walk away. Sometimes you might need a lifeguard to help get you back to shore. There's no shame in that.

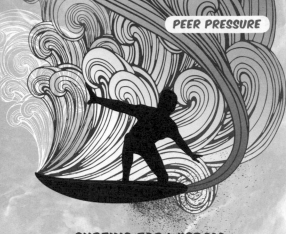

SURFING FOR WISDOM

It is the LORD your God you must follow, and him you must revere. Keep his commands and obey him; serve him and hold fast to him.
Deuteronomy 13:4

[Jesus began to teach them, saying]: Everyone who hears these words of mine and puts them into practice is like a wise man who built his house on the rock. The rain came down, the streams rose, and the winds blew and beat against that house; yet it did not fall, because it had its foundation on the rock.
Matthew 7:24–25

Oh, the joys of those who do not follow the advice of the wicked, or stand around with sinners, or join in with mockers. But they delight in the law of the LORD.
Psalm 1:1–2 NLT

To those who by persistence in doing good seek glory, honor and immortality, he will give eternal life.
Romans 2:7

LIFE SAVER

DIVING FOR UNDERSTANDING

Stand up for what is right
even if you are standing alone.
Anonymous

To be nobody but yourself, in a world which is doing its best,
night and day, to make you everybody else, means to
fight the hardest battle which any human being
can fight; and never stop fighting.
E.E. Cummings

LIFE SAVER CHALLENGE

I will combat peer pressure in my life with these methods:

1. Choosing friends who value the same things I do.

2. Practicing saying "No" the next time I'm invited to do something I'm not comfortable doing.

3. Asking God in prayer to give me the courage not to follow the crowd.

MANNING THE LIFE BOAT

At one time or another, everyone is a leader and a follower. There are people in your life that may be following you. Where are you leading them? Name two people who look up to you and for whom you can try to become a leader worth following:

1.

2.

SAIL ON IN PRAYER

God,
Sometimes it feels so much easier to
just go along with what everyone else is doing.
I don't like confrontation, and I don't always feel
strong enough to say "No" to people in my life.
I don't want to feel left out and left behind.
Show me how to stand firm for what I believe.
I believe You are the source of
courage—encourage me!
Amen.

PERSEVERANCE

PADDLING FAST IN A LEAKY CANOE

Water wears away stones.
Job 14:19

"And the winner is…" Just a year earlier, Sammy Jo Claussen would never have believed her name would follow those four words. After all, Sammy Jo was the "loser." A high school senior, Sammy Jo only read at a fourth grade level. Struggling with dyslexia, bipolar disorder, ADD, and anger issues, Sammy Jo kept her classmates and her family at arm's length. Sammy Jo felt as if she couldn't do anything right—except cook.

So that's what Sammy Jo did. In a local Teen Chef competition, participants were asked to create one dish. Sammy Jo whipped up an entire meal. Her win sent her to regionals. A week before the competition, Sammy Jo broke her wrist bowling. But she didn't quit. Though she couldn't move her wrist, she competed in knife skills, as well as cooking, and won again—by one point. Sammy Jo worked with a professional chef on time management, organization, and cooking skills to prepare for nationals. But it was perseverance, along with Sammy Jo's pan-fried catfish, that won the Teen Chef competition and a $90,000 college scholarship for her. Despite her learning challenges, Sammy Jo continues to persevere toward her culinary arts degree at a college in Kansas.

When you feel like a failure, it's easier to give up than to keep trying. But with God's help, you can find the strength you need to face every challenge that comes your way. Each morning is a brand-new start. Any failures or setbacks are in the past. Ask God what steps you can take toward your goal today. Then, persevere.

CATCHING THE WAVE

Diligence is like running a marathon: staying focused on your goal and pushing yourself to make it as fast as you can to the end of the course. Perseverance is similar. But this time, picture that course filled with hurdles. Perseverance is diligence in the face of tough times and setbacks. When people persevere, like Sammy Jo Claussen, they not only work hard, they also work through hard things. They don't give up, despite difficulties, discouragement, and disappointment. As long as they believe God is saying, "You can do it," they continue to move forward, one step at a time.

SURFING FOR WISDOM

We do not give up. Our physical body is becoming older and weaker, but our spirit inside us is made new every day.
2 Corinthians 4:16 NCV

Let's not allow ourselves to get fatigued doing good. At the right time we will harvest a good crop if we don't give up, or quit.
Galatians 6:9 MSG

You need to persevere so that when you have done the will of God, you will receive what he has promised.
Hebrews 10:36

The testing of your faith develops perseverance. Perseverance must finish its work so that you may be mature and complete, not lacking anything.
James 1:3-4

Blessed is the man who keeps on going when times are hard.
James 1:12 NIrV

LIFE SAVER STORY

Derby told us how she persevered:

"I've had trouble with cutting. Then I went back to God, and it was all good. Then a friend committed suicide recently, and I started up again. I even thought about suicide because the hurt was so much. I felt like, if he did it, then why can't I? But I realized that's not the way to go. God designed us for a purpose, and He created us in His image; that is the most beautiful thing ever in the world. Go to a friend for help ... maybe even go to Jesus. But get help. I did; even though I'm tempted at times to cut again and give up, I don't. The easy thing isn't always right. Do what is right. Live your life and don't give up ... ever."

Have you ever felt like giving up? Did you find the strength to persevere? What is your story?

_____

_____

_____

_____

_____

_____

_____

_____

_____

_____

WHAT IT ALL MEANS

per·se·ver·ance: n. (pur-suh-veer-uhns)

Steady persistence in a course of action, a purpose, a state, etc., esp. in spite of difficulties, obstacles, or discouragement.

4 REASONS TO PERSEVERE

1. God has a plan and a purpose for your life.

2. Your life is valuable—no matter what anyone says.

3. You are stronger than you think.

4. Nothing has ever been solved by quitting.

LIFE SAVER

DIVING FOR UNDERSTANDING

Nobody trips over mountains. It is the small pebble that causes you to stumble. Pass all the pebbles in your path and you will find you have crossed the mountain.

Anonymous

Perseverance is the hard work you do after you get tired of doing the hard work you already did.

Newt Gingrich

Look at a stone cutter hammering away at his rock, perhaps a hundred times without as much as a crack showing in it. Yet at the hundred-and-first blow it will split in two, and I know it was not the last blow that did it, but all that had gone before.

Jacob A. Riis

LIFE SAVER CHALLENGE

I will practice perseverance by following these five steps:

1. Celebrate every morning as a fresh start.

2. Place yesterday's failures or disappointments in God's hands.

3. Ask God to show me what I can learn from my setbacks.

4. Review what I hope to accomplish today that will help me move forward.

5. With God's help, do my best today without holding on to yesterday or worrying about tomorrow.

MANNING THE LIFE BOAT

Use the buddy system to persevere through tough times. Write specific prayer requests on a 3 x 5 card, and then ask someone who knows you well to pray for these requests. Check in at least once a week, sharing how you've seen God at work and updating your requests. Return the favor by asking how you can pray for your friend.

SAIL ON IN PRAYER

Lord God,
I can't persevere without You.
I get tired and discouraged when things
fall apart. But I know You can give me
the strength and the creativity
I need to make it past any hurdles in my way.
Please stay close to my side.
I need You.
Amen.

POTENTIAL
MAKING WAVES

**[Jesus said,] "Anything is possible
if a person believes."**
Mark 9:23 NLT

When Rachael Flatt first stepped onto the ice at the age of three, no one really pictured her as an Olympic champion. But soon everyone could see that she was magic on the ice. By the time she entered high school, she had become a world-class figure skater and a contender for the U.S. Olympic team. The bright, 17-year-old, straight-A student with an impressive work ethic proved her mettle at the 2010 U.S. Figure Skating Championship in Spokane, Washington. It was there that she became the first U.S. woman to break 200 points, bringing home a personal best short program and free skate. The title won her a place on the U.S. Olympic team and the thrill of competing in the 2010 Winter Olympic Games in Vancouver, British Columbia.

As her Web site will attest, Rachael has a lot of fans and admirers. You might even be one of them. It's tempting to look at this young woman and think, *I wish I had that kind of potential.*

You may not be as uniquely gifted as Rachael, but God has endowed you with unique gifts and abilities as well. The key to living up to your potential lies in trying new things and then putting your newly discovered gifts and abilities to use. The only way Rachael discovered she was a gifted figure skater was by lacing up her skates and stepping out on the ice. After that it was a matter of working hard and staying at it.

You won't find your special gift by sitting in your room watching television or listening to iTunes. You have to get out there and try new things until you discover where your magic lies.

CATCHING THE WAVE

Potential comes from the Latin word for "power." That means God has given you the power to make the most of what you've been given. Your gift might bring you fame and fortune, or it may result in the love and respect and appreciation of those who are touched by your life. Your power begins with self-discovery—finding out what your gifts and talents might be. Then with God's help, hard work, and determination, you too can achieve far more than you ever imagined.

SURFING FOR WISDOM

[Jesus] said to them, "... Truly I tell you, if you have faith the size of a mustard seed, you will say to this mountain, 'move from here to there,' and it will move; and nothing will be impossible for you."
Matthew 17:20–21 NRSV

I have filled him with the Spirit of God, with skill, ability and knowledge in all kinds of crafts.
Exodus 31:3

Each one should use whatever gift he has received to serve others, faithfully administering God's grace in its various forms. If anyone speaks, he should do it as one speaking the very words of God. If anyone serves, he should do it with the strength God provides, so that in all things God may be praised through Jesus Christ.
1 Peter 4:10–11

God's gifts and his call are irrevocable.
Romans 11:29

LIFE SAVER

DIVING FOR UNDERSTANDING

Everyone has inside of him a piece of good news.
The good news is that you don't know how great you can be!
How much you can love! What you can accomplish!
And what your potential is!

Anne Frank

We are all gifted. That is our inheritance.

Ethel Waters

The potential of the average person is like a huge ocean unsailed,
a new continent unexplored, a world of possibilities waiting
to be released and channeled toward some great good.

Brian Tracy

LIFE SAVER CHALLENGE

I will work to fulfill my potential by:

1. Making a list of things that interest me and stir my passions.

2. Trying new things, even if they carry me outside my comfort zone.

3. Working hard to become the best that I can be.

4. Refusing to limit what God can do through me.

MANNING THE LIFE BOAT

People, especially young people, are often blind to their own strengths and giftings. You can help others identify their gifts and move toward reaching their potential by offering words of encouragement when you recognize something special in someone else. Let them know what you see. Make yourself available to listen to their thoughts and ideas. Support them in prayer.

SAIL ON IN PRAYER

Almighty God,
All too often I place limits
on what You can do in me and through me.
Please show me what my gifts and abilities are,
and then give me the courage to put them
into practice. Help me believe in myself
as much as You believe in me.
Amen.

PURPOSE
SWIMMING IN THE RIGHT DIRECTION

The LORD will fulfill his purpose for me.

Psalm 138:8

Some people just know what their purpose is. Olympic gold-medal swimmer Amanda Beard says that as a young child she often joked that she would be swimming in the Olympics one day. Somehow she just knew. Zach Hunter was just 12 years old when he launched Loose Change to Loosen Chains, a student-led effort to raise awareness of modern-day slavery. No one asked him to stand up for the enslaved of the world. It was a natural response to what he felt in his heart.

Amanda and Zach make it look easy, but for most of us, finding our purpose is a bit trickier. There aren't any earth-shattering realizations, no sense of intense inner knowing. We come to it slowly over time. Sometimes we don't get it until we're looking back on years already lived.

You may be quite certain about what you were created to do and be, or you may be shrugging your shoulders right now and admitting you don't have a clue. Either way, you can be sure that God has a purpose for your life just as He has for Amanda and Zach. It may not include taking home Olympic gold or speaking on behalf of the estimated 27 million slaves in the world, but God's purpose for your life will be every bit as important. Just keep swimming in the right direction— doing your best, learning all you can, listening to the people who love you, and staying close to God. One day you'll look around and know—just know—this is what you were meant to do.

CATCHING THE WAVE

The Bible says God created each of us with a specific plan and purpose in mind. It isn't something to obsess about or worry over. It's all about opening up your heart to God and listening to Him speaking to you through the Bible and those who care about you. He may choose to reveal your purpose all at once or a little at a time. It may be dramatic and earth shaking, or it may be quiet and precious and little known. You'll know by the inner joy and peace it brings you. Even though it may be difficult or painful at times, you'll feel good, complete, and fulfilled when you are walking in God's perfect purpose for you

SURFING FOR WISDOM

"I know the plans I have for you," says the LORD. "They are plans for good and not for disaster, to give you a future and a hope."
Jeremiah 29:11 NLT

It's in Christ that we find out who we are and what we are living for.
Ephesians 1:11 MSG

We know that in all things God works for the good of those who love him, who have been called according to his purpose.
Romans 8:28

Each one has his own gift from God, one in this manner and another in that.
1 Corinthians 7:7 NKJV

DIVING FOR UNDERSTANDING

We must not, in trying to think about how we can make a big difference, ignore the small daily differences we can make which, over time, add up to big differences that we often cannot foresee.
Marian Wright Edelman

Be daring, be different, be impractical, be anything that will assert integrity of purpose and imaginative vision against the play-it-safers, the slaves of the commonplace, the creatures of the ordinary.
Cecil Beaton

Don't ask yourself what the world needs; ask yourself what makes you come alive. And then go and do that. Because what the world needs is people who have come alive.
Harold Whitman

LIFE SAVER CHALLENGE

I will pursue my purpose with these five steps:

1. Talking to God every day about His plan for my life.

2. Seeking advice from my parents and the other adults God has placed in my life.

3. Being open to new ideas and new opportunities and trying new things.

4. Letting my heart tell me what I love to do.

5. Reminding myself daily that God created me with a purpose, and He is committed to helping me find it.

MANNING THE LIFE BOAT

No matter what purpose God has for your life, it will include reaching out in some way and helping others. Name two things you would enjoy doing in the service of others.

1.

2.

— SAIL ON IN PRAYER —

Lord God,
Thank You for my life.
I want to make it count for something
good by following the plan You have
prepared for me. I admit the world often seems
confusing. It's hard to be sure of anything.
But I know You are there watching over me,
helping me, and showing me the way.
I promise to follow You,
one step at a time.
Amen.

RESPECT

STORM SURGE

Those who respect the Lord will have security.

Proverbs 14:26 NCV

"I'd like you to explain why you gave me a C. I don't get Cs," Ana said, tossing her paper on her English teacher's desk.

Mrs. Chesney took her time looking up. "I didn't *give* you anything, Ana," she answered. "You earned your grade."

"You can't be serious," she persisted. "I deserve at least a B."

Mrs. Chesney took a breath, turned to face Ana, and spoke in a calm, authoritative tone. "Ana, the grade stands. I'd be happy to talk to you about how to improve in my class, but I suggest for now you take some time and rethink your approach. When you're ready to speak to me in a respectful tone, we'll talk again."

Ana's mouth dropped open. Then she turned and headed for the door. "Forget about it," she called back over her shoulder. "Some teacher you turned out to be."

The next morning Ana arrived at class a few minutes early and quietly approached Mrs. Chesney's desk.

"I'm sorry for how I acted yesterday," she said when her teacher looked up from the paper she was grading. "I get A's—only A's. I didn't know what to do with a C."

"I get that; really I do," said Mrs. Chesney. "And I'm willing to do everything I can to help you get that C up to an A. But I won't tolerate disrespect. Are we clear?"

Ana nodded.

"Now, what do you say we start over?" Mrs. Chesney said. "Bring me your paper, and I'll show you what you can do better next time."

CATCHING THE WAVE

Respect is more than just a word. It's an attitude accompanied by appropriate actions. God expects you to show respect not only for Him but also for all those in authority over you. And not only for those in authority, but also for each and every person, simply because we were all created in His image. In so doing, you ensure that you will have a proper respect for yourself. And respecting yourself will give you the strength to stand up for yourself and avoid careless choices with unfortunate consequences.

SURFING FOR WISDOM

Knowledge begins with respect for the LORD, but fools hate wisdom and discipline.
Proverbs 1:7 NCV

Give to everyone what you owe them: Pay your taxes and government fees ...., and give respect and honor to those who are in authority.
Romans 13:7 NLT

We ask you ... to respect those who work hard among you, who are over you in the Lord and who admonish you. Hold them in the highest regard in love because of their work.
Live in peace with each other.
1 Thessalonians 5:12-13

Wisdom begins with respect for the Lord; those who obey his orders have good understanding.
Psalm 111:10 NCV

DIVING FOR UNDERSTANDING

Respect is love in plain clothes.
Frankie Byrne

Respect your fellow human being, treat them fairly, disagree with them honestly, enjoy their friendship, explore your thoughts about one another candidly, work together for a common goal and help one another achieve it.
Bill Bradley

Every human being, of whatever origin, of whatever station, deserves respect. We must each respect others even as we respect ourselves.
Ralph Waldo Emerson

LIFE SAVER CHALLENGE

I will learn to respect myself by:

1. Showing respect for God as my Creator, for His commandments, and for His constant presence in my life.

2. Showing respect for those God has placed as authorities in my life to teach me how to be the person He created me to be.

3. Showing respect for every person created in His image.

MANNING THE LIFE BOAT

Do you owe someone an apology because you have
failed to give them the respect they were due?
If so, make it right.
Your actions will set things right in your life
and serve as an example to others.

--- SAIL ON IN PRAYER ---

God,
Help me to respect even those
whom I may not always agree with.
Help me to remember that You have placed
people in authority over me for my own good.
I will trust You to help me do the
right thing at all times.
Amen.

SELF-ESTEEM
THE TIDES OF INSECURITY

Before I formed you in the womb I knew you, before you were born I set you apart.
Jeremiah 1:5

David Ring was born dead. But that wasn't the end of his story. David was revived, but his brain had gone so long without oxygen that he developed cerebral palsy, a disorder that affects muscle control and coordination. Throughout his teen years, David suffered from physical pain and frequent ridicule. Then, both of his parents died. At 14, David was an orphan bounced from one temporary home to another. Discouraged and depressed, David dropped out of school. Things looked hopeless, but once again David was about to find new life.

At 17, David began to understand how much God loved him. As his faith grew, David's self-esteem grew right along with it. He graduated from high school and then college. During this time, he began speaking at churches, schools, and conventions. More than 30 years later, David continues to travel the world as a motivational speaker, telling audiences, "I have cerebral palsy, but cerebral palsy doesn't have me."

Lots of people are disabled in this life. David is not one of them. Cerebral palsy makes it difficult for David to speak clearly. But knowing that God created him for a purpose gives David the confidence he needs to speak in front of thousands of people.

Is there anything disabling you? Maybe you're shy. You have a lisp. Your parents are divorced. You don't feel as smart as your peers. But whatever makes you feel small or self-conscious in front of others doesn't have to be a stumbling block. God can help you use it as a stepping-stone that leads deeper into the adventure of living a confident, courageous life.

CATCHING THE WAVE

True self-esteem is seeing yourself through God's eyes. It means you're aware of your strengths and your weaknesses, your victories and your failures. It also means you realize that your worth and influence are greater than the sum of all those things. When you reach out to God, His power works in your life, enabling you to do more than you ever could on your own. That's what turns self-confidence into God-confidence. As you trust in God's power to work through you, you'll begin to take hold of the confidence you need to face any challenge that comes your way

SURFING FOR WISDOM

The LORD shall be thy confidence,
and shall keep thy foot from being taken.
Proverbs 3:26 KJV

Know that the LORD is God.
It is he who made us, and we are his; we are
his people, the sheep of his pasture.
Psalm 100:3

You made all the delicate, inner parts of my
body and knit me together in my mother's
womb. Thank you for making me so
wonderfully complex! Your workmanship is
marvelous—how well I know it.
Psalm 139:13-14 NLT

[Jesus said,] "Are not two sparrows sold for
a penny? Yet not one of them will fall
to the ground apart from the will
of your Father. And even the very hairs
of your head are all numbered.
So don't be afraid;
you are worth more than many sparrows."
Matthew 10:7.9-31

LIFE SAVER

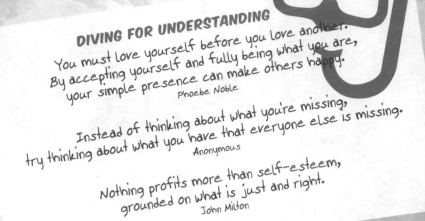

DIVING FOR UNDERSTANDING

You must love yourself before you love another.
By accepting yourself and fully being what you are,
your simple presence can make others happy.
Phoebe Noble

Instead of thinking about what you're missing,
try thinking about what you have that everyone else is missing.
Anonymous

Nothing profits more than self-esteem,
grounded on what is just and right.
John Milton

LIFE SAVER CHALLENGE

I will build up my God-confidence by reviewing these five truths each day:

1. **God knew me even before I was born.** *(Psalm 139:13)*
2. **God designed me with a special purpose in mind.** *(Jeremiah 29:11)*
3. **God can use everything in my life to bring about something good.**
   (Romans 8:28)
4. **Nothing can separate me from God's love.** *(Romans 8:38–39)*
5. **Even death is not the end of my story.** *(John 3:16)*

MANNING THE LIFE BOAT

Be generous with words of encouragement. When people do a good job or look as if they could use a friendly "Way to go!" risk trying something difficult, and speak up. Build their self-esteem with your praise and their God-confidence by sharing the truths you're reviewing each day.

SAIL ON IN PRAYER

Lord God,
I believe in You.
Please help me believe in myself.
Not because I want to trust in my own abilities,
but because I want to trust that with You
I can face any challenge that comes my way.
Give me the courage and confidence I need
to move ahead.
Amen.

SEX & TEMPTATION
STAYING OUT OF HOT WATER

When you are tempted, [God] will also provide a way out so that you can stand up under it.
1 Corinthians 10:13

Here's a bit of advice that you might not expect to find in a book from a Christian publisher: You need to think about sex more. Really.

This doesn't mean swapping off-color jokes with friends, trolling for porn on the Internet, or entertaining lustful feelings for some hottie at your school. It does mean serious, thoughtful, and yes, prayerful consideration.

Why? Consider this: One of the primary reasons teens succumb to sexual temptation is that the topic isn't talked about openly in settings that can shed light and wisdom on the challenges and choices of it. It makes us feel uncomfortable. Just the same, we *have* to talk about it, because sexual temptation is real. In our world, it's everywhere you look.

You need to think about sex, because your attitude and actions (or lack of actions) will profoundly affect your future. For example, the best wedding gift you can give your future spouse is a lack of sexual baggage dragged into your marriage. (A Colorado marriage-counseling service notes that the No. 1 reason for strife in the couples they counsel is the guilt, shame, suspicion, jealousy, and insecurity caused by one or both partners' sexual activity before marriage.)

The New Testament book of Philippians contains some great advice: It advises us to think about things that are *noble, right, pure, lovely, admirable, excellent, and praiseworthy*. Sexuality, when it's lived out according to the One who invented it, is all of the above and more. Think about that, especially the next time you're tempted. And when you have questions, ask the adults in your life until they agree to help you find the answers.

CATCHING THE WAVE

To help clarify the answer to the age-old question, "How far is too far?" try this exercise. *Before* you find yourself in a potentially sexually compromising situation, imagine your future spouse—somewhere out in the world—in that *same exact* situation. Now, think about what you'd want your future spouse to do.

Guys: Are you okay with some guy kissing your future wife the way you intend to kiss your current girlfriend? Girls: Are you okay with some girl touching your husband-to-be the way you are thinking about touching your boyfriend? Kind of clears up the whole "How far?" question, doesn't it?

SURFING FOR WISDOM

It is God's will that you should be sanctified: that you should avoid sexual immorality; that each of you should learn to control his own body in a way that is holy and honorable, not in passionate lust like the heathen, who do not know God ... For God did not call us to be impure, but to live a holy life.
1 Thessalonians 4:3-5, 7

Among you there must not be even a hint of sexual immorality, or of any kind of impurity, or of greed, because these are improper for God's holy people.
Ephesians 5:3

There is a sense in which sexual sins are different from all others. In sexual sin we violate the sacredness of our own bodies, these bodies that were made for God-given and God modeled love, for "becoming one" with another.
1 Corinthians 6:18 MSG

Everything in the world—the cravings of sinful man, the lust of his eyes and the boasting of what he has and does—comes not from the Father but from the world. The world and its desires pass away, but the man who does the will of God lives forever.
1 John 2:16-17

DIVING FOR UNDERSTANDING

To go into temptation to find how strong you are, is as wise as to go before a mirror, with closed eyes, to find how you look when asleep.
Ivan Panin

Flee temptation and don't leave a forwarding address.
Anonymous

The first characteristic of sexual sin is deceit. It never delivers what it promises. It offers great satisfaction but gives great disappointment. It claims to be real living but is really the way to death.
John MacArthur

LIFE SAVER CHALLENGE

To resist sexual temptation, I will:

1. Avoid Web sites, TV shows, or any media that might feed me unhealthy sexual thoughts and images.

2. Set clear, specific sexual boundaries and discuss them openly with the person I'm dating.

3. Avoid scenarios that might put me in a compromising sexual situation (e.g., unsupervised parties, events where alcohol is served, or a significant other's house when no one else is around).

4. Find a youth pastor, friend, or other mature person I can talk with openly—and who will keep me accountable to standards of healthy sexuality.

5. Remind myself that being a Christian will NOT protect me from the consequences of disobeying God's standards for sex—consequences like pregnancy, STDs, and a damaged reputation.

MANNING THE LIFE BOAT

True, sex might not be the most comfortable conversation-starter for sharing your faith. But, on the other hand, if sex is the topic, you can be pretty sure you'll have a captive audience. And people you talk with will likely be intrigued—and pleasantly surprised—when you inform them that God isn't some giant sexual buzz-kill. This thing was His idea, and all His ideas are good.

SAIL ON IN PRAYER

Dear God,
You invented sex,
and You invented it to be an awesome thing
between two people truly in love and fully
committed to each other forever. Help me to resist
the temptations that seem to be everywhere
these days. Help me to be patient,
remembering always that the best sex
in the world is sex that is lived out
according to Your plan.
Amen.

WISDOM
IMPROVING YOUR STROKE

Whoever listens to [wisdom] will live in safety and be at ease, without fear of harm.
Proverbs 1:33

When students at Summit Middle School need advice, somehow they find their way to Luke Miller, who often offers a different perspective on any problem. But that hasn't always been the case. "For most of my life, I didn't want anyone telling me what to do," he comments as he leans back in his chair. "I'd sneak out of the house to play with my friends. Then my parents would catch me and ground me. I hated being stuck in my bedroom, but then I'd sneak out of the house again, and get grounded again.

"Finally, on one of those perfect days when I'd much rather be outside skateboarding—but I was stuck in my room—I looked at myself in the mirror and said, 'Luke, why do you keep banging your head against the wall? If you'd learn from your mistakes, your life would get better.' Everything changed after that. It's funny, because some people think I'm a 'wise guy' or something. When they come to me with their problems, I just ask lots of questions and then ask them, 'What can you learn from this?' Anyone can do that."

To be wise like Luke, just be willing to learn—from your mistakes, other people's mistakes, and other people in general. Of course, it's most important to learn from God, because all wisdom comes from Him! It also requires some humility, because you have to admit that you don't know everything. But you will definitely enjoy the life God has planned for you when you decide to grow in wisdom.

CATCHING THE WAVE

Wisdom is the ability to
successfully apply what
you know to everyday life.
This book is intended to be
a tool to help you learn to
be wise. It contains wise
principles from the Bible,
which is the ultimate guide
to wisdom. The Bible says
Jesus grew in wisdom—in
other words, He became
wiser and wiser as He grew
up. If you want to be like
Jesus, ask God for wisdom;
He has promised to gener-
ously share it with you.

SURFING FOR WISDOM

Wisdom is a tree of life to those who
embrace her; happy are those who
hold her tightly.
Proverbs 3:18 NLT

If any of you lacks wisdom, he should ask
God, who gives generously to all without
finding fault, and it will be given to him.
James 1:5

Get wisdom, get understanding; do not forget
my words or swerve from them.
Do not forsake wisdom, and she will protect
you; love her, and she will watch over you.
Wisdom is supreme; therefore get wisdom.
Though it cost all you have, get understanding.
Proverbs 4:5-7

Doing wrong is like sport to a fool,
but wise conduct is pleasure to a person
of understanding.
Proverbs 10:23 NRSV

The wisdom that comes from heaven is first
of all pure; then peace-loving, considerate,
submissive, full of mercy and good fruit,
impartial and sincere.
James 3:17

215

LIFE SAVER

DIVING FOR UNDERSTANDING

The next best thing to being wise oneself
is to live in a circle of those who are.
C. S. Lewis

We seem to gain wisdom more readily
through our failures than through our successes.
We always think of failure as the antithesis of
success, but it isn't.
Success often lies just the other side of failure.
Leo F. Buscaglia

Wisdom consists of the anticipation of consequences.
Norman Cousins

LIFE SAVER CHALLENGE
I can grow in wisdom by following these three steps:

1. Reading one chapter out of Proverbs every day (there are 31 chapters for 31 days in a month).

2. Starting a wisdom notebook where I'll jot down my favorite verses from Proverbs and the lessons I'm learning from my life and the lives of other people.

3. Memorizing two or three of my favorite verses from my notebook.

4. Asking God to share some of His wisdom with me.

MANNING THE LIFE BOAT

You can help other people grow in wisdom too. Name two ways you can do this.

1.

2.

SAIL ON IN PRAYER

Dear God,
You know so much, and I know so little.
I want to be like Jesus and grow in wisdom.
So would You share some of Your amazing wisdom
with me so I can be more like You?
Please give me the humility to look at my life
with an open heart, and show me the difference
between wisdom and foolishness.
Amen.

WORDS
CRASHING WAVES

[Jesus said,] "A good person produces good things from the treasury of a good heart."

Matthew 12:35 NLT

Have you ever squeezed a stubborn tube of toothpaste from the middle, sending a foot-long "toothpaste snake" slithering across your sink? The problem with a mishap like this is that once the toothpaste is out of the tube, it's out for good. No amount of coaxing, manipulating, or prodding will change that.

Words, like toothpaste, are unretractable. Once hasty, hurtful words are spoken, you can't take them back. The best you can do at that point is deal with the consequences. Picture the following scene. Someone says something mean to you. You demand that the person take it back, but it isn't happening. So you go for her hair or push him to the ground and sit on him. These drastic techniques might win you a desperate, "OK, OK! I take it back. Just get off of me!" But both of you know the words can't really be taken back. They've been spoken, and the damage has been done.

Of course, positive, encouraging words are equally powerful. For some reason, we tend to leave those unspoken, trapped behind our lips where they don't do anyone any good. Every day we can choose words that heal rather than wound; inspire rather than discourage; comfort rather than defeat; build up rather than tear down.

What we say matters. Words make an immediate, lasting impact for good and for harm. God has given you complete control over the words that come from your mouth. No one can take that from you. How will you use your words?

CATCHING THE WAVE

When you brush your teeth in the morning, think of that act as a reminder to choose your words carefully during the day ahead. When you brush your teeth at night, do a "word inventory." How did you do? Did you, as the Bible urges, "speak the truth in love"? Did your words tear down or build up? Did you exercise your power for good or for harm? Did you speak words of encouragement, kindness, joy, peace, and love? Were your words pleasing to your heavenly Father? Never forget that your words may be the only thing in your world that you have complete control over.

SURFING FOR WISDOM

What you say can mean life or death. Those who speak with care will be rewarded.
Proverbs 18:21 NCV

When you talk, do not say harmful things. But say what people need—words that will help others become stronger.
Ephesians 4:29 ICB

Let the words of my mouth and the meditation of my heart be acceptable in Your sight, O LORD, my strength and my Redeemer.
Psalm 19:14 NKJV

Be gracious in your speech. The goal is to bring out the best in others in a conversation.
Colossians 4:6 MSG

Whoever would love life and see good days must keep his tongue from evil and his lips from deceitful speech.
1 Peter 3:10

DIVING FOR UNDERSTANDING

Words. Do you fully understand their power? Can any of us really grasp the mighty force behind the things we say? Do we stop and think before we speak, considering the potency of the phrases we utter?
Joni Eareckson Tada

Cold words freeze people, and hot words scorch them, and bitter words make them bitter, and wrathful words make them wrathful. Kind words soothe, and quiet, and comfort the hearer.
Blaise Pascal

Words—so innocent and powerless as they are, as standing in a dictionary, how potent for good and evil they become in the hands of one who knows how to combine them!
Nathaniel Hawthorne

LIFE SAVER CHALLENGE

I will make my words count for good by:

1. Making it a practice to think before I speak.

2. Taking time to pray and meditate before a difficult conversation with someone.

3. Refraining from saying anything when I'm not sure what to say. (There's probably a good reason for my hesitation.)

4. Exercising extreme caution and restraint when it comes to speaking when I'm angry, overtired, frustrated, or all of the above.

5. Asking myself, before speaking, "How would I like to hear the words I'm about to say?"

MANNING THE LIFE BOAT

If you can be a dependable source of encouraging words, lots of people will want to hear what you have to say. For some people in your circle—your school, your church, your neighborhood—you may be the only one who speaks positive, encouraging, life-giving words into their lives. Imagine what a difference you could make!

SAIL ON IN PRAYER

Dear God,
I can still feel the sting
of unkind words,
even those spoken to me years ago.

Help me to say words that encourage,
heal, and enlighten.
May my words always flow from a heart
that is devoted to You.
Amen.

221

WORRY & ANXIETY
WATER WORKS

I want you to be free from anxieties.
1 Corinthians 7:32 NRSV

"I don't know what to say," Cameron said.

"It doesn't matter what you say. What matters is that you're there," his mother encouraged.

"I'm not good at this touchy-feely stuff," Cameron protested. "He'll understand if I don't go."

"Just be there. The words will come when you need them," his mother said.

"I just don't want to make it worse," he said.

"Don't worry," she said. "That's like saying one more drop of water would make the ocean wetter. Not possible."

Cameron could not relate to what Tyler must be going through. He couldn't imagine what it would be like to wake up one morning and find out your dad is dead. It would be easier if Tyler was just another kid at school and not his best friend. It would be easier to walk away.

"Just ask yourself what's the worst that could happen if you go in there. And remember that it's really not about you," his mother said.

Worry is personal. What worries you may not faze someone else. But God has heard it all. No matter how big or how small your problem is, you can take it to Him and be certain that He can handle it. But He may ask you to do one thing in return—trust Him with what you're worrying about and let Him take care of it.

CATCHING THE WAVE

The Bible says that you don't have to worry about tomorrow or even the next five minutes! Sometimes you may find that you worry more about what you can't control than what you can. There are some circumstances that you can't change and others you will need to ask God to help you accept. For those that can be changed, you will need to ask God to show you how to change worry into action. The key is to take every worry, every concern to God first.

SURFING FOR WISDOM

[Jesus said:] "Give your entire attention to what God is doing right now, and don't get worked up about what may or may not happen tomorrow."
Matthew 6:34 MSG

[Jesus said,] "Do not worry about your life, what you will eat or what you will drink, or about your body, what you will wear. Is not life more than food, and the body more than clothing? Look at the birds of the air; they neither sow nor reap nor gather into barns, and yet your heavenly Father feeds them. Are you not of more value than they?"
Matthew 6:25-26 NRSV

Trust in the LORD with all your heart and lean not on your own understanding; in all your ways acknowledge him, and he will make your paths straight.
Proverbs 3:5-6

DIVING FOR UNDERSTANDING

Blessed is the person who is too busy
to worry in the daytime
and too sleepy to worry at night.
Author Unknown

Every evening I turn my worries over to God.
He's going to be up all night anyway.
Mary C. Crowley

There is a great difference between worry and concern.
A worried person sees a problem,
and a concerned person solves a problem.
Harold Stephens

LIFE SAVER CHALLENGE

I will turn my worries over to God by:

1. Asking God to show me what is worth worrying about and what isn't.

2. Stepping out with courage to do those things that scare me the most.

3. Remembering that I don't have to keep what I worry about to myself;
   I can confide in someone who loves me.

4. Remembering that trusting God is a process. What I struggle with today
   will seem much easier as I grow in my faith.

MANNING THE LIFE BOAT

Sometimes when you worry too much, you might miss caring for the needs of others in your life. Is there someone whose worry might be even greater than your own? Write the name of that person or persons below, and then commit to praying for their worries to flee and their trust in God to grow:

1.

2.

SAIL ON IN PRAYER

God,
You know that I worry about things I can do little or nothing to change. Help me to take every worry and turn it into a prayer instead. Help me to not worry about what I should wear or what I should eat, and focus instead on trusting You to show me the way.

Help me to also not cause undue worry to others in my life.
Let my life become a worry-free zone.
Amen.

WORSHIP
WAVES OF PRAISE

You shall worship the LORD your God.
Exodus 23:25 NRSV

Whom do you worship? That may sound like a trick question. After all, worship seems like such a churchy word. Worship is when people sing on Sunday mornings. Worship is when people get on their knees and pray. Worship is what people do for God. But worship can also be following your favorite celebrity on Twitter. It can be screaming yourself speechless as your favorite band enters the concert arena. It can be going out of your way to become friends with the star of the football team.

At its heart, worship is devotion. When you wholeheartedly devote your attention, your emotions, and your energy to something or someone, you form an attachment. At times, that attachment can cross over into worship. Only you and God know when you cross that line.

You were made to worship. It's natural for you to feel the pull to look up in awe at someone greater than yourself. But the only Someone who truly qualifies for worship is God. When you aren't focused on God and devoted to Him, it's easy to slide right into worshipping something else—something that makes you feel powerful or desirable. It may be a person, someone you dream will love you for who you are. It may be a thing, like money or a new car, something you feel will make you valuable in the eyes of others. Your true value and your greatest love are found in God alone. Only He is truly worthy of your worship. Only He will live up to and exceed your expectations. Only He will never disappoint you.

CATCHING THE WAVE

Worshipping God is more than singing songs on Sunday morning or praying before meals. To worship God means to invite Him to be involved in every area of your life. That sounds kind of scary, like giving up control. The truth is, that's exactly what it means. But God knows you better, and loves you more deeply, than anyone else ever will. When you choose to use your words, your actions, and even your body in ways that honor Him, you not only worship God, you also do the most awesome thing you can ever do for yourself and your future.

SURFING FOR WISDOM

I will thank you forever, because of what you have done. In the presence of the faithful I will proclaim your name, for it is good.
Psalm 52:9 NRSV

O come, let us worship and bow down, let us kneel before the LORD, our Maker!
For he is our God, and we are the people of his pasture, and the sheep of his hand.
Psalm 95:6-7 NRSV

The hour is coming, and is now here, when the true worshipers will worship the Father in spirit and truth, for the Father seeks such as these to worship him. God is spirit, and those who worship him must worship in spirit and truth.
John 4:23-24 NRSV

All the ends of the earth shall remember and turn to the LORD; and all the families of the nations shall worship before him. For dominion belongs to the LORD, and he rules over the nations.
Psalm 22:27-28 NRSV

LIFE SAVER

DIVING FOR UNDERSTANDING

The worship of God is not a rule of safety—it is an adventure of the spirit.
Alfred North Whitehead

Worship isn't listening to a sermon, appreciating the harmony of the choir, and joining in singing hymns! It isn't even prayer, for prayer can be the selfish expression of an unbroken spirit. Worship goes deeper.

Since God is spirit, we fellowship with him with our spirit; that is, the immortal and invisible part of us meets with God, who is immortal and invisible.
Erwin W. Lutzer

Worship means "to feel in the heart."
A. W. Tozer

LIFE SAVER CHALLENGE

I will worship God in these five ways:

1. Ask God to show me any idols I have in my life.

2. Ask Him to help break any attachments I have to these idols.

3. Begin each day with prayer, to help focus my thoughts on God.

4. Generously share what I have with others, remembering that everything I have is a gift from God.

5. Get involved in a local church where I can learn more about what true worship means.

MANNING THE LIFE BOAT

You can worship God all on your own. But getting involved in a church youth group can help your relationship with God to grow in fresh, new ways. One way of worshipping God is loving others well. Refuse to just hang out with your friends. Reach out to the new kids or those who like to stay on the sidelines.

--- SAIL ON IN PRAYER ---

Lord God,
You are the Creator of everything,
including me. Your power is far greater
than I could ever imagine, but so is Your love.
Show me how to worship You by living my life
in a way that makes You smile.
Help me fall more deeply in love
with You each day.
Amen.

FOREVER

LIFE SAVER CERTIFICATION

God sent not his Son into the world to condemn the world; but that the world through him might be saved.

John 3:17 KJV

"Josh, what happened to you over the summer?" Ben asked. "You seem so different. I know you weren't getting into trouble, but you seem so much more … peaceful."

"Ben," Josh replied, "I had the most awesome summer of my life. I went to camp with Joey's youth group. We jumped off some cliffs into a lake and went whitewater rafting. But the best part was the camp speaker. He talked about Jesus as if He was his best friend. He told us, 'It doesn't matter what's happened in your life; the moment you give your life to Jesus, you get to start over.' It's kind of like rebooting your heart.

"So one night at camp, I rebooted—and I gave my life to Jesus. Ben, I feel so clean inside!"

If you haven't already given your life to Jesus, you can do it right now. It doesn't mean your problems will suddenly disappear or you won't have any more struggles. But it *does* mean you have a new best friend who will never leave you. He'll wipe away all your sins and guide you through all the dark places in your life. All you need to do is admit your sin to Jesus, ask Him to forgive you, and tell Him that you want Him to be in charge. Then He promises to forgive you and reserve a place in heaven where you can spend eternity. Sounds almost too good to believe, but it's true!

CATCHING THE WAVE

Two thousand years ago, the world's only perfect man was crucified on a cross. The Bible says that God demonstrated His love for us by sending His Son, Jesus, to tell us about His Father's love and show the world how everyone can be forgiven. Most amazing of all, you don't have to do anything to earn salvation. When you give God your sin, He gives you eternal life in return. Even though it seems like a one-sided deal—God promises to honor it!

SURFING FOR WISDOM

All the prophets testify about him that everyone who believes in him receives forgiveness of sins through his name.
Acts 10:43

Once made perfect, [Jesus] became the source of eternal salvation for all who obey him.
Hebrews 5:9

If you confess with your mouth, "Jesus is Lord," and believe in your heart that God raised him from the dead, you will be saved. For it is with your heart that you believe and are justified, and it is with your mouth that you confess and are saved.
Romans 10:9-10

Christ was sacrificed once to take away the sins of many people; and he will appear a second time, not to bear sin, but to bring salvation to those who are waiting for him.
Hebrews 9:28

DIVING FOR UNDERSTANDING

A person may go to heaven without health, without riches, without honors, without learning, without friends, but he can never go there without Christ.
John Dyer

It is not your hold of Christ that saves you, but his hold of you!
Charles Spurgeon

My salvation was a free gift. I didn't have to work for it, and it's better than any gold medal that I've ever won.
Betty Cuthbert

LIFE SAVER CHALLENGE

I will follow Jesus by following these five steps:

1. Getting involved in a church with a youth group where I can learn more about God and meet people who share my faith in Jesus.

2. Reading my Bible, starting in the book of Mark.

3. Talking with God every day.

4. Telling a friend I trust about my decision.

5. Dedicating the rest of my life to following Jesus.

MANNING THE LIFE BOAT

You can introduce other people to Jesus too. Name
two people you would like to tell what has happened to you.

1.

2.

— SAIL ON IN PRAYER —

Dear Jesus,
We both know that
I'm not a perfect person.
Please forgive my sins
and take control of my life.
Thank You for giving Your life
for me—now I give my life to You.
I can't wait to see the places
we'll go together.
Amen.

ABOUT THE AUTHORS

"I love helping teenagers dig into God's word," **Michael J. Klassen** explains. "It's like taking vitamin supplements for the soul." Since 1997, he has worked on 25 Bibles and contributed to numerous books for teenagers.

A father of three teenage daughters—and a former teenager himself—he has first-hand experience dealing with youth issues. Michael currently pastors The Neighborhood Church in Littleton, Colorado, and leads the church middle school group with his wife Kelley.

Michael's Web site is http://bibleconversation.wordpress.com/michaeljklassen-com/.

Vicki Caruana has worked as a high school to college advisor, a coordinator of a middle school gifted magnet school, and (now) teaches at the college level. Vicki is also the mother of two college-age sons and is personally engulfed in their everyday struggles. As a high school youth minister at her church, Vicki works with teens on a daily basis to help them navigate how to live this life in a way that is full of love, friendship, success and honor.

Vicki is the author of more than 20 books, which include the best selling *Apples & Chalkdust* and *Giving Your Child the Excellence Edge*. Vicki lives with her husband in Seminole, Florida.

Vicki's website is www.vickicaruana.blogspot.com.

Todd Hafer is an award-winning writer with more than 30 books to his credit. His teen/young adult novel *Bad Idea* was a Christy Awards finalist in the Youth category, and its sequel, *From Bad to Worse*, was named one of the top-ten books of the year by Christian Fiction Reviews.

Battlefield of the Mind for Teens, which he co-wrote with Joyce Meyer, has been a best-seller on both the Christian Retailing and CBA lists and recently reached number one on Amazon.com's Teen/Spirituality best-seller list. He also collaborated with Don Miller on *Jazz Notes: Improvisations on Blue Like Jazz*.

Parents of four teenagers and one wayward rescue dog, Todd and his wife JoNell, live in Shawnee Kansas.

Todd's Web site is: www.haferbros.com.

Vicki Kuyper has written more than fifty books, including *Jesus Speaks to Teens* and *Wonderlust: A Spiritual Travelogue for the Adventurous Soul*. Her latest release is *Breaking the Surface: Inviting God into the Shallows and Depths of Your Mind*.

Vicki has worked on a wide variety of projects for companies such as Integrity Music, the International Bible Society, NavPress, Willow Creek, and Compassion International. She's also written numerous magazine articles, book reviews, video scripts, greeting cards, and the occasional cow-pun calendar. When Vicki isn't writing, she often speaks at women's retreats and special events.

Vicki and her husband Mark live in Phoenix, Arizona. They have two adult children who not so long ago were teens.

Vicki's Web site is: www.vickikuyper.com.

LIFE SAVER

Follow the To Save A Life story in novel #2, **JAKE'S CHOICE!**

NEW!
JAKE'S CHOICE
(available late October 2010)

THE SECOND NOVEL IN THE *TO SAVE A LIFE* SERIES

Having graduated from high school with a newfound faith and a basketball scholarship, Jake Taylor heads to Louisville to begin life as a college student. Thousands of miles separate him from his girlfriend Amy Briggs, and they find their lives moving in very different directions. Befriending a young girl with a traumatic history leads Amy back to the father who abandoned her. Jake's position on the Louisville basketball team lands him in the midst of parties, beautiful women ... and one decision that will shake him to the core. When everything Jake believes is challenged, will he go with the flow or stand alone for what is right? One choice will change everything ...

TO SAVE A LIFE

Based on the screenplay for the movie, the *To Save A Life* novel includes scenes and back stories not shown in the film.

TO SAVE A LIFE:
DARE TO MAKE YOUR LIFE COUNT

A powerful, inspirational book for teens based on the message in the movie, *To Save A Life*.

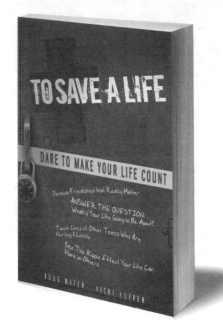

+DEVELOP friendships that really matter

+ANSWER THE QUESTION: What is your life going to be about?

+TOUCH LIVES of other teens who are hurting and lonely

+SEE THE RIPPLE EFFECT your life can have on others